Our Spiritual Inheritance

By Ed Skidmore

Our Spiritual Inheritance

By Ed Skidmore

Copyright © 2012 by Ed Skidmore

ISBN 978-1-61529-059-8

Vision Publishing
1672 Main Street E 109
Ramona, CA 92065
1-800-9-VISION

www.booksbyvision.com

All rights reserved worldwide

No part of the book may be reproduced in any manner without the written permission of the author except in brief quotations embodied in critical articles of reviews.

Unless otherwise indicated, All Scripture taken from the Holy Bible New International Version. Copyright 1973, 1978, 1984, International Bible Society. Used by permission of Zondervan Publishing House. All rights reserved.

Acknowledgements

To my favorite professor and lifetime friend, Wallace Wartick, who read through my manuscript and gave me tremendous advice to help me teach these principles with greater clarity and a better understanding of my likely audience, I appreciate the participation so willingly provided, and the attention to detail which proved that he gave this matter his full attention.

To Mike Daniel of S.A. Stone Ministry, my pastoral coach for the past two years, who has been working on his own book while reading through mine and providing encouragement, and advice to enable this book to survive the rigors of writing, editing, and revising to make it all the way to the publisher's desk, I give my appreciation and admiration.

To my wife, Susan, the unscrupulous modifier of all things literary, I give a boat-load of gratitude for being the other set of eyes on the project that came her way when many other things were on her plate. Thanks for helping me give birth to this book.

Dedication

To my patient, and loving wife of 40 years,
and my two wonderful daughters
who have provided us with admirable sons-in-law
and absolutely amazing grandchildren,
I dedicate my second book,
with hope that it will be a source of encouragement
for growing Christians in many places.

Table of Contents

Introduction: Our Spiritual Inheritance 5

Chapter 1: What does the New Testament
    say about our Inheritance? 9

Chapter 2: Wrapped up in God 19

Chapter 3: The Covenant Origin of our Inheritance 31

Chapter 4: The Indwelling Presence of the Holy Spirit 37

Chapter 5: The Power to Overcome 47

Chapter 6: God's Unique Relationship to Each of Us 57

Chapter 7: Joint Heirs with Christ 65

Chapter 8: The Authority in the Name of Christ 71

Chapter 9: The Glory of Christ: Past Present and Future 81

Chapter 10: Appropriating our Inheritance by Faith 89

Chapter 11: Life in the Kingdom 95

Chapter 12: Defend your Inheritance! 101

Chapter 13: A Case Study in Dual Inheritance 109

Chapter 14: Our Future Inheritance 115

Chapter 15: Passing on Our Inheritance 121

Appendix A: Inheritance Passages in
    the New Testament 125

Introduction: Our Spiritual Inheritance

Many years back when our family moved to San Antonio we lived, for about six months, in a rented Condominium. We picked our temporary lodging primarily because it was economical and close to the church I serve as pastor. We moved in knowing about the covered parking for my two cars, and about the three outside storage closets which we filled with our belongings. But because we hadn't actually talked to the owner of the condo, there were other amenities we were not aware of, and didn't take advantage of for the first couple of months living there.

As the weather warmed up, we looked for places where the kids could swim, and paid to use public pools. About two months into our time at the condo, the little girl next door invited our girls to go swimming with her at the condo pool. Condo Pool? We had never heard anything about a pool at our condo, but about two blocks away, there it was, and it was ours to use freely.

Meanwhile, every week my wife would head out with the family laundry to a coin operated Laundromat. Two hours and several stacks of coins later, she would come home lamenting the loss of the use of her own washer and dryer which were parked in the aforementioned storage areas. Months had gone by when I walked through the kitchen one day and noticed something in the wall that looked familiar. I don't know why I hadn't noticed before, but it certainly looked like a normal washer hook up, near the downstairs half bath. On closer examination, there was a hot and cold water shut off and a place to put a washer drain line.

Yep, it was a place to hook up our washer alright. We quickly retrieved our machine from storage and hooked it up. Voila! Then when we looked outside on our enclosed patio for a way to hook up a clothesline, surprise! There was a 220 hookup for a dryer. It seemed a little unconventional to place a dryer outside in the weather, but, when we hooked it up there, it worked. We simply covered it with a canvas tarp to keep it from rusting in the elements.

Our reasonably priced condo had amenities we were not aware of, and therefore, did not enjoy, for part of the time we lived there. Our nice, reasonably priced condo, became a terrific palace after we learned about the features that came along with the condo itself. We were glad to learn about the extras, but we wished we had known about them from the day we moved in.

This unexceptional little experience of ours points to the purpose for which I write this book. We as Christians are recipients of a "glorious inheritance" (Ephesians 1:18) because of our connection to God. Unfortunately, many believers are not aware of all that is included in that inheritance. Some actually become Christians simply to escape the fires of hell. There is so much more to our life with God, than just taking out fire insurance against infernal damages. Like our discoveries while living in our condo, believers who take the time to look beyond just the "pearly gates" can discover many other features of our spiritual inheritance. Our walk with God can go beyond "nice" to "glorious".

I have chosen to use the word "inheritance" to describe the wonderful blessings God has showered upon us because we belong to him. I found that word used dozens of times in the New Testament to explain what God has promised and provided to those who are His. This book will uncover, chapter by chapter, the rich and glorious inheritance God has in store for his people. My hope is that those who learn about what God has promised and is providing will grow in their love for God, will dedicate themselves more fully to his service, will abide in Christ more intimately, and will allow Jesus to live his life within them daily.

Who can benefit from taking the time to read through the pages of this book?

- Anyone who wants to grow in their spiritual walk will find plenty of resources to assist them in the transformation from infancy to rooted and grounded growth. (Colossians 2:7)

- Anyone who feels alienated from God and is convinced that he will never measure up to God's standards. (Ephesians 2:8-9, Hebrews 9:15)

- Anyone who is not sure why there is anything to be gained from making a commitment to connect with God and to accept His offer of salvation. (John 3:16-18)

- Anyone debating about the goodness and compassion of God. (James 1:16-18)

- Anyone seeking to know the truth about God, but knowing next to nothing about the claims of Christianity.

- Anyone stuck in neutral in his spiritual walk who wants to be shifted into "drive".

- Anyone who is not sure whether or not God even exists. (Hebrews 11:6)

- Anyone…

Chapter 1: What does the New Testament say about our Inheritance?

Key Verses: Ephesians 1:18-19, *"I pray also that the eyes of your heart be enlightened in order that you may know the hope to which he has called you, the riches of his glorious inheritance in the saints, and his incomparably great power for us who believe. That power is like the working of his mighty strength."*

The general subject of inheritance can often bring out both good and bad emotions. I can remember, through the years, hearing about families torn apart when certain members felt that they were unfairly shorted in the doling out of inheritance. For example, I remember a former neighbor whose only valuable asset was a piece of property about 5 acres in size. He had 10 children and step children on whom he wished to bestow his property. In an effort to be fair to all, he simply portioned out the property in half acre strips of land measuring about 50 feet by 350 feet.

I was told that the ungrateful children's greatest complaint was over who had to share a boundary with whom. Certain children didn't want land next to certain step children. It apparently did not occur to anyone that a 50 foot wide strip of land was uninhabitable. Perhaps the benefactor would have been wiser if he had sold the property and portioned out the money to each child. This example confirmed for me the lesson that inheritance can be a bitter or sweet experience depending on the attitude of the benefactor as well as the attitudes of the recipients.

At this point in my life I have physically inherited one thing. It is a gold pocket watch handed down to me from my great grandfather, James Texter Fink. I do not remember having ever met the man, but it is meaningful to me that a remembrance from him was passed on to me. This token of relationship helps me connect back to former generations in my family. Furthermore, it is something I want to pass on to one of my grandsons when he becomes an adult. I am glad to receive an inheritance, and look forward to passing it along to the next generation. Likewise, our spiritual inheritance is a treasure to share with other believers.

Everyone loves the idea of receiving an inheritance, whether large or small. However, many Christians fail to perceive the glorious spiritual inheritance that is ours through Christ Jesus. This spiritual inheritance is not merely for our future enjoyment, but is available to us here and now.

Looking at the key verse for this chapter, we notice the Apostle Paul praying that the Christians in Ephesus would be enlightened to know the hope to which they have been called, the riches of his glorious inheritance in the saints, and the power for us who believe (Ephesians 1:18-19). To be enlightened implies that we do not discover these things merely by intellectual means. Enlightenment requires divine revelation. The Holy Spirit must reveal these things to us. My hope is that readers of this book will be enlightened and thus lay hold of this glorious spiritual inheritance.

The New Testament mentions the subject of inheritance in association with the kingdom of God surprisingly often. Searching through the New Testament text, I found 45 references to this topic (see Appendix A). In the process of my study, I was also surprised to find very little written about the subject of spiritual inheritance in books or magazines. Because of the dearth of available information I have taken the time to study what the Bible says about inheritance, and I uncovered a wealth of inspiration and encouragement for the growing Christian who might be curious about all that God has provided to those who belong to Him.

The subject of inheritance is peppered throughout the Bible. In the Old Testament inheritance generally refers to land and other possessions passed on from one generation to another, but even there, we notice a spiritual component present that transcends the concept of earthly possessions.

In the New Testament, the subject of inheritance is almost exclusively spiritual in nature. As children of God we become inheritors of the promises of God and participants in the covenants of God. We interact with God the Father, God the Son, and God the Holy Spirit in ways that connect us to deity beyond anything that worldly religions can promise. This element of inheritance alone is worthy of our full attention. Therefore, we will give considerable attention to it.

The New Testament speaks of an inheritance God has set aside exclusively for believers. What do these passages reveal to us about our inheritance from God? We will allow the text to introduce us to the nature of our spiritual inheritance in this chapter. This will also serve as the springboard for the rest of the topics we will cover. What can we learn about our spiritual inheritance from the New Testament texts?

1. **This inheritance is granted among all who are sanctified:** In the Apostle Paul's farewell address to the Ephesian elders he uttered this final benediction to those he loved. Acts 20:32 records, *"Now I commit you to God and to the word of his grace, which can build you up and give you an inheritance among all those who are sanctified."* We notice that the inheritance is shared by those who are sanctified. From this we may conclude that this blessing is enjoyed by those who share a relationship with God, and by implication, denied to those who are not in God's family (See Chapter 2).

2. **The inheritance depends on God's promise:** Paul takes the time to differentiate between what the law provides, and what God promised to Abraham before the Mosaic Law was ever given. He wrote in Gal 3:18, *"For if the inheritance depends on the law, then it no longer depends on a promise; but God in his grace gave it to Abraham through a promise."* We discover that God's promise of an inheritance to Abraham, which included both land and descendants, was an unconditional promise based on an everlasting covenant which preceded God's covenant with Israel. That same promise is also available to us as Christians for we are also descendants of Abraham. (Romans 4:16, Galatians 3:6-14) (See Chapter 3).

3. **This inheritance is related to a new covenant:** In Hebrews 9:15 we notice that Jesus is a mediator of a new and different covenant based on his death. We read, *"For this reason Christ is the mediator of a new covenant, that those who are called may receive the promised eternal inheritance – now that he has*

died as a ransom to set them free from the sins committed under the first covenant." Jesus is actually the testator of a new will which was put into effect after his death on the cross. Our inheritance is based on His finished work and completed redemption (See Chapter 3).

4. **The Holy Spirit is a deposit guaranteeing our inheritance:** Apostle Paul assures us that, *"...Having believed, you were marked in him with a seal, the promised Holy Spirit, who is a deposit guaranteeing our inheritance until the redemption of those who are God's possession- to the praise of his glory" (Ephesians 1:13b-14).* The presence of the Holy Spirit living within us is like a down payment on all that God has promised to provide to those who are His. Because He is there, we know that there is more to come (See Chapter 4).

5. **Our inheritance includes the power to overcome everything that might attempt to defeat us:** The Apostle John had much to say about overcoming, and in the book of Revelation there were special messages given to overcomers in Revelation chapters 2 and 3. All that is included in the letters to the seven churches is summed up in Rev. 21:7 where John writes, *"He who overcomes will inherit all this, and I will be his God and he will be my son."* Our inheritance includes tremendous power to live continuously in victory (See Chapter 5).

6. **We inherit a unique, "one of a kind" connection with a Heavenly Father who knows each of us intimately and plans out our lives ahead of time according to his eternal purposes:** *Psalm 139:13-18, "For you created my inmost being; you knit me together in my mother's womb. I praise you because I am fearfully and wonderfully made; your works are wonderful, I know that full well. My frame was not hidden from you when I was made in the secret place. When I was woven together in the depths of the earth, your eyes saw my unformed body. All the days ordained for me were written in your book before one of them came to be. How precious to me are your thoughts, O God! How vast is the sum of them! Were I to count them, they would outnumber the grains of sand. When I awake, I am still with*

you." I rejoice in knowing that my connection with God is unique, and not a "One size fits all" relationship. No two of us are exactly alike, and God treats each one of us uniquely and individually (See Chapter 6).

7. **As children of God we are heirs, and co-heirs with Christ:** Romans 8:17 reminds us that with son-ship comes the right of heirs: *"Now if we are children, then we are heirs – heirs of God and co-heirs with Christ, if indeed we share in his sufferings in order that we may also share his glory."* Our inheritance comes as a result of our son-ship to Our Heavenly Father, and our brotherhood with Christ. Having shared in His sufferings we are promised that we will also share in His glory. Paul goes on to explain in Galatians 3:29 that because we belong to Christ we also inherit the promise given to Abraham because we are also his seed. *"If you belong to Christ, then you are Abraham's seed, and heirs according to promise."* Though it might be logical to conclude that only natural born Jews could claim such a promise, Paul states clearly that Gentiles share with the Jews in all promises through Christ. *"This mystery is that through the gospel the Gentiles are heirs together with Israel, members together of one body, and sharers together in the promise in Christ Jesus."* (Ephesians 3:6)(See Chapter 7).

8. **The church has been given the name of Jesus Christ, and the authority of that name to use in ministry:** Jesus, speaking to his disciples at the last supper gave them this promise in John 14:13-14, *"And I will do whatever you ask in my name, so that the Son may bring glory to the Father. You may ask me for anything in my name, and I will do it."* As a part of our connection to Jesus Christ he has given us his name to use in our ministry on earth. This is a part of our inheritance as joint heirs with Christ. Jesus was an heir to his Father's promises, and we, as Christ's followers share in that same inheritance as joint heirs. (Romans 8:17) (See Chapter 8).

9. **We inherit the transformational power of Christ's Glory which changes us into His likeness:** In 2 Corinthians 3:18 where we are told, *"And we, who with unveiled faces all reflect the*

Lord's glory, are being transformed into his likeness with ever-increasing glory, which comes from the Lord, who is the Spirit." The glory of Jesus has the ability to transform us into the likeness of our master if we behold that glory with no veils covering our eyes. We are changed from one degree of glory to the next by the Holy Spirit. (See Chapter 9)

10. **This inheritance is a reward of faithful service:** We see that our inheritance is related to our connection to and activity in behalf of the God we serve. Colossians 3:24, *"...since you know that you will receive an inheritance from the Lord as a reward. It is the Lord Christ you are serving."* Though some are inclined to wonder why our actions on God's behalf have anything to do with our inheritance, this is consistent with Christ's words in Matthew 25:34-45 about the actions and words of those on the right and left of the King in the parable of the sheep and goats (See Chapter 10 and 12).

11. **Believers inherit the Kingdom:** Jesus is speaking about the judgment day when he says, In Matthew 25:34, *"Then the king will say to those on his right, 'Come, you who are blessed by my Father; take your inheritance, the kingdom prepared for you since the creation of the world.'"* From this passage we see that those who are saved (on his right) inherit the kingdom which has been prepared for them since the creation of the world. This means that it has always been God's plan to provide the kingdom which Jesus preached during his public ministry on earth. We will learn what it means to live our lives within that kingdom (See Chapter 11).

12. **It is possible through immorality or godlessness to give up our inheritance:** The writer of Hebrews warns against setting aside our inheritance in favor of lesser things. We read in Hebrews 12:16, *"See that no one is sexually immoral, or is godless like Esau, who for a single meal sold his inheritance rights as the oldest son."* Looking at the account in Genesis 25:27ff, we notice Esau giving up his birthright for a bowl of red beans. The birthright of the firstborn son in a family was no small matter. To the firstborn would go a double portion of inheritance

and the right to be executor of the father's estate. For Esau to "despise" his rights as firstborn (vs. 34) revealed how little he valued his rightful inheritance. We also treat our inheritance from God as worthless through sin and rebellion (See Chapter 12).

13. **A case study concerning inheritance:** Luke 15 gives an example of our dual inheritance (both physical and spiritual) from the parable of the prodigal son who came to his father with this demand in vs. 12, *"The younger one said to his father, 'Father, give me my share of the estate.' So he divided his property between them."* From this fascinating example of Jesus' teaching we are allowed to look into the life of the son who was only interested in his physical inheritance, and had to learn about his spiritual inheritance in the process of losing all his earthly assets. (See Chapter 13).

14. **Our inheritance is eternal:** Peter writes how God has given us new birth into a living hope through Christ's resurrection, and goes on to explain the following*: "and into an inheritance that can never perish, spoil or fade – kept in heaven for you,"* (I Peter 1:4). The events of the last several years (2008-2009) have proved that retirement savings can take a major hit regardless of where they have been invested. Even seemingly conservative investments dropped suddenly in the fall of 2008. So much for careful planning and shrewd investments. Juxtaposed to these shaky times, God has given an inheritance that can never *"perish, spoil or fade."* And the reason for that permanence is that it is kept in heaven for us (See Chapter 14).

15. **This is a rich inheritance:** By revelation we are enabled to know all that God has provided to us. Paul wrote, *"I pray also that the eyes of your heart may be enlightened in order that you may know the hope to which he has called you, the riches of his glorious inheritance in the saints." (Ephesians 1:18)* What we receive from God is not miniscule in its size and scope. It is far beyond anything we might inherit from earthly parents. Our spiritual

inheritance is far greater than any physical inheritance we might receive (See Chapter 14).

From what we see above, we are able to uncover the astounding bounty we inherit both while we are here on earth and when we will eventually arrive in our heavenly home. This study of our spiritual inheritance takes us far beyond merely escaping the fires of hell, or entering the gates of heaven. Our inheritance includes so much more than just "pie in the sky, by and by." In fact, we are heirs to so many present and future treasures that we can't possibly catalogue them all, but we can give thanks to God for all that he has bestowed upon us in his mercy and grace.

Questions to consider:

1. Have you ever inherited anything from a family member?
2. Have you taken steps to pass something on to another person by making a will?
3. Of all the things we can learn about our inheritance from God, which of these discoveries is most surprising to you?
4. What do you think is the most important reason for focusing on the study of our inheritance from God?
5. As you read these pages, are you willing to echo the Apostle Paul's prayer in Ephesians 1:18-19 and ask for the eyes of your heart to be enlightened to know the hope to which God called you, the riches of God's glorious inheritance in the saints, and God's incomparably great power for us who believe?
6. What constitutes a spiritual inheritance and how does it differ from a physical inheritance?
7. Is this spiritual inheritance available to everyone regardless of their spiritual condition? (Acts 20:32)
8. What is the connection between our inheritance and God's promise and why is that important? (Galatians 3:18)
9. Why is the Holy Spirit called a down payment (earnest KJV) on our inheritance? (Ephesians 1:13-14)
10. What is the relationship between our inheritance and the kingdom of God? (Matthew 25:34)

Chapter 2: Wrapped up in God

Key Verses: 1 Peter 1:3-4, *"Praise be to the God and Father of our Lord Jesus Christ! In his great mercy he has given us new birth into a living hope through the resurrection of Jesus Christ from the dead, and into an inheritance that can never perish, spoil or fade – kept in heaven for you,"*

Back in my youth ministry days I taught the teen-agers a simple song that packed a theological wallop. The words to the chorus went like this:

I'm just wrapped up, tied up, tangled all up in Jesus.

I'm just wrapped up, tied up, tangled all up in God (Repeat both lines)

(Danny Lee, 1972, Manna Music).

It was not only fun to sing along with the actions, (and the faster the better,) but the message of our multi-faceted connectedness to God was a lesson worth repeating.

We humans tend to be rather insecure about most things, and when it comes to spiritual connection with God we are prone to wonder whether we are in or out of the *"assembly of the righteous"* (Psalm 1:5). Knowing our propensity to doubt our inclusion in God's family, he has taken great pains to explain our connectedness to himself with multiple metaphors peppered throughout the Bible. Surely, an important aspect of our inheritance as Christians is that of seeing how completely we are wrapped, tied, and tangled all up in God. Consider these examples:

- God has purchased us with Christ's blood making us his possession (Ephesians 1:14)
- He adopted us into his family making us his children (Romans 8:15)
- He planted in us the "incorruptible seed" of his Holy Spirit giving us his DNA (1 Peter 1:23)

- He betrothed us to his Son causing us to become the Bride of Christ (Revelation 22:17)
- He is the potter and we are the clay (Romans 9:21)
- Jesus is the foundation of a building and we are living stones in that same building (1 Peter 2:5)
- Jesus is the great shepherd and we are his sheep (John 10:11-16)
- Jesus is our leader and we are soldiers in his army (2 Timothy 2:3-4)
- Jesus is the high priest and we are a holy nation of priests (Hebrews 4:14, 1 Pet. 2:9)
- Jesus is the vine and we are the branches (John 15:1-8)
- Christ is the head and we are his body (Ephesians 1:22, 5:30)
- Christ is the authority and we are his disciples (Matthew 28:18-20)

When I visited Russia in 1996 I purchased a Matrioshka or "Nesting" doll which is perhaps one of the most commonly purchased Russian souvenirs. I had no idea how popular this toy would be with my grandchildren. They have played with it so much that we have had to tape some of the dolls back together to keep the toy intact. The nesting doll provides a good visual image of the ways we have been wrapped up in Christ and in God. The common nesting doll contains seven dolls starting with a large doll that comes apart in the middle revealing a smaller doll inside, and each doll comes apart to reveal a yet smaller doll until you discover the smallest doll, about the size of a pea. As you put them back together you understand that the smallest doll is covered up and protected six times over.

Consider how, in the same manner, we are covered up at least twice over. Colossians 3:1-3 reminds us, *"Since, then, you have been raised with Christ, set your hearts on things above, where Christ is seated at the right hand of God. Set your minds on things above, not on earthly things. For you died, and your life is now hidden with Christ in God."* Like the nesting doll, we are hidden in Christ, and both of us are hidden in God.

Looking at the various ways God has chosen to connect us to himself should be very reassuring to otherwise insecure humans. Let us then focus on some of the various ways God has wrapped us up in himself:

We are God's sons and daughters

This is a twofold connection because both ways of becoming God's children are mentioned in the New Testament text. There is an adoption and also a spiritual begetting and birthing. Both of these processes make us into God's sons and daughters, but there is a shade of difference between them we shouldn't miss.

The adoption element of our connection to God comes because we are not born physically into God's family at birth. The default condition for each of us is that of being a child of Adam's race. By nature, we inherited our DNA from Adam and Eve who, by means of their sin, separated themselves from God. We are born into the human family as natural men and women. This concept is presented by the Apostle Paul in Romans 5:12-20 letting us know that through one man, sin and death came to all men, but through the obedience of one man, Jesus Christ, the gift of grace was made available to all mankind potentially.

I used the word potentially, because there must be a receiving of that grace for it to become effective. There is a big difference between Christianity, where salvation is to be received in order for it to be effective, and Hinduism, which teaches that receiving God would be unnecessary because everyone has some aspect of a god living in them already. The Hindu's only need is to look inside himself to discover what is already there. Contrary to the Hindu concept of pantheism (god is everywhere), the Bible teaches that God is a transcendent Spirit, who loves mankind and has lovingly provided a way, through his unique Son, to bring us back to himself. A much-needed grace is offered freely as a gift to whoever desires to receive it. And by means of receiving that gift, God provides His Holy Spirit, which is called a "Spirit of adoption, whereby we cry Abba, Father!" (Romans 8:15). The Spirit God placed within us enables us to call God by the familiar name which in Aramaic would be "Abba" and in the English idiom would come closest to "Daddy!"

The whole meaning of adoption is that a loving person would take a child who was not naturally born to him and, by choice, do whatever is needed to make them into an offspring with all the same rights and privileges as a naturally born child. Though they do not share DNA, they will consequently share all other familial connections from that point on. By adoption, the child becomes a son or daughter of the adopting parent and a brother or sister to any other natural born siblings. He inherits anything the parent chooses to pass on to the adopted child. Once again, the significance of adoption is to take someone not naturally born in a family and place them into the family by choice of the adoptive parent. And this choosing by the parent would also imply a willingness by the child to be chosen for adoption. So far, in the natural realm, I've never heard of anyone being adopted who protested their adoption.

The Apostle Paul gave another metaphor similar to that of adoption when he talked about grafting Gentiles onto the tree that had once been exclusively Jewish (Romans 11:17-24). The idea there was that branches from a wild olive plant were grafted onto the Jewish rootstock because of their faith, while some natural branches were lopped off due to unbelief. What was not native to the original rootstock was grafted by choice of the owner of the olive tree. Can you see the similarity between adoption of a child into an established family and grafting of a branch onto a developed rootstock? Both adoption and grafting reveal God's willingness to take what was not his own by nature (from birth) and to make it his own.

Perhaps you are aware of a common interest adopted children have to know who their natural "birth parents" are. Especially those who were adopted at birth will develop a curiosity sooner or later about the people who brought them into the world in the first place. Even though they may adore their adoptive parents, they can't help but wonder about their natural parents.

God had a remedy in mind to deal with this possibility. He didn't stop with adoption in his interest to connect with his chosen offspring; he did something else only He could do. He planted his own DNA into those who became his by faith. Where would an idea like that come from? Look at 1 Peter 1:23, *"For you have been born again, not of perishable seed, but of imperishable, through the living and enduring word of God."* The word used in the Greek text for seed is the word "sperma" from which we get our word "sperm." When we talk about being "born again" we are referring to the fact that God begets and births new life in those he saves. He plants his own Holy Spirit into our spirits, which is the implantation of His own godly nature within us.

Consider the following passages which state the case for our begetting, birthing, and being a new creation in connection to God: John 1:12-13; John 3:3, 7; 2 Corinthians 5:17; Galatians 6:15; 1 Peter 1:3, 23; 1 John 5:1, 18. Leave it to our loving and understanding Father to do everything possible to make us fully his children. I love the way John put it in his gospel introduction, John 1:12-13, *"Yet to all who received him, to those who believed in his name, he gave the right to become children of God – children born not of natural descent, nor of human decision or a husband's will, but born of God."*

Spiritual begetting and birthing is so much more than just ascribing intellectual assent to the tenants of a religious system, or putting one's name on the membership roll of a local church congregation. We literally become new creatures with a godly nature along with a spiritual presence enabling us to do God's will (2 Corinthians 5:17; Philippians 2:13). Furthermore, we are secure in our connection to God. Having made us into His children, God is not about to un-adopt us or to un-birth us from his family. We are able to call God, "Daddy!" all the days of our lives with confidence that our place in his family is secure.

We are Saints

This next connection we have with God is not as easy to visualize as that of being a child of God. One of the reasons for that is that the institutionalized church, to describe people of special merit or status in the church, has held the word "saint" hostage. The common conception of saint is that of a person who is somehow better than the average believer. For example, Catholics will grant sainthood post mortem to people of superlative merit, like perhaps a Mother Theresa type of worker in the church. Sometimes miracles or martyrdom are involved in the decision to grant sainthood.

Certainly, with that concept of saint in vogue, no one sitting in a pew would have the boldness to take such a title as "saint" upon themselves. We're ok with being believers, disciples, servants, followers, church members, congregants, Christians, even children of God; But saints? We consider that to be presumptuous at best.

What a surprise, then, to find out that the New Testament uses that term to describe people who belong to Christ. Notice how the Apostle Paul used two phrases side by side to describe one group of people. Referring to the judgment day which is to come when Christ returns, Paul wrote in 2 Thessalonians 1:10 (KJV), "*...when he comes on that day to be glorified in his Saints, and to be marveled at in all who have believed.*" Both phrases, "his Saints", and "all who have believed," refer to the same people. In fact, every place where the word "saint" or "saints" is used refers to believers in Christ. To read it any other way is to misunderstand what the author was conveying in the New Testament passage.

Coming from the Greek word "hagios" and the Hebrew word "qadosh" or "chesed" this word can refer to saints, holy ones or things, set apart, special, different, or consecrated. Though this word was used in New Testament times to refer to believers in the church, it did not lose the meaning of "holy ones" when referring to them. It is no casual matter for the writers of the Bible to use this term in the way it was used. God sees his people as special, set apart ones. In the same way that certain clothing, vessels, tools, and furniture were set apart to special purposes in the time of the tabernacle and temple, the members of God's house in the New Testament time and beyond, are also holy and set apart to special purpose and value.

Calling Christians "saints" is not a mistake on God's part, nor is it just a mind game to make Christians feel better about themselves. "Saints" is what God calls us because saints is what we are. God declares us righteous because of the finished work of Christ who redeemed us and sanctified us. Positionally, we are holy people. It is also true that because the Holy Spirit resides within us in our spirits, we have holy DNA (so to speak.) Therefore, the trend in our lives is towards ever increasing holiness in our wills and behavior. We may not get there overnight, but from one degree of glory to the next we are being transformed into the likeness of our Savior and King whose glory we behold with unveiled face, nothing keeping us from seeing Him as he is. 2 Corinthians 3:18

This is quite a departure from the "worm theology" so often taught in the church, which would describe us with such terms as "a wretch like me" or "such a worm as I." I know that John Newton, who used one of those phrases to describe himself in the song, "Amazing Grace" was thinking back to his former days as the captain of a slave trading ship, and a reprobate sinner. But, I am confident that Newton was also well aware that he was no longer a wretch as a consecrated member of God's family.

I sometimes hear believers referring to themselves as "sinners saved by grace." Though there is a sense in which that is true as they look back on their former hopeless condition, it is not a proper representation of their current position in God's family. God would not call us saints if all we are now is "sinners" with a pardon. We know that God doesn't lie, so if He calls us saints, then saints we most certainly are.

Some may ask, "But what if I don't always act like a saint?" An occasional lapse into un-saintly behavior does not change our position in God's kingdom, nor does it negate our inherited new nature. It is simply a wakeup call to slumbering saints who have allowed the corpse of the "old man" as Paul describes him, to sneak out of the grave where he has been placed. Therefore, it is our task to "mortify" the old, dead, former self and consign that ugly zombie back into his grave. In fact, Paul writes about a song that was evidently sung at baptisms in the early church. Consider these words, *""Wake up, O sleeper, rise from the dead, and Christ will shine on you."* Ephesians 5:14. Seeing Christ in his glory enables us to be transformed into the same image day by day (2 Corinthians 3:18) so that we become more saintly in our behavior as we grow in His likeness.

We are Sheep and Christ is our Good Shepherd

I know that some may see this sub-heading as a step backwards in looking at all the ways we have been wrapped up in God. It is true that sheep are not the brightest lights in the animal kingdom. It is easy for a sheep to get itself lost without even trying. All a sheep has to do is chew its way from clump to clump of grass, and when it finally looks up, "Where did the flock go?" One thing can be said for sheep though; they know how to follow their leader. Give a sheep a good leader, and the sheep will be happy, healthy, protected, and provisioned in every way possible. King David, himself a former sheepherder, wrote a wonderful poem about the provision of the good shepherd in Psalm 23. Jesus also expounded on his role as the good shepherd in John 10:1-29.

In contrast to Christ's words, we can look back to Ezekiel 34 where God told Ezekiel to prophecy against Israel's shepherds *(her leaders) who were "fleecing the flock" so to speak*. God promised to come in himself as the good shepherd to remove the wayward shepherds, and to provide better care for them than Israel's leaders had been providing. What would be the purpose for this metaphor concerning our connection to God? I believe that if we are paying attention to the way things are going in our lives, we will sooner or later come to an awareness of our need for God's watch-care, guidance, and provision. We are more like sheep than we want to admit. And we need the good shepherd to lead us more than we will ever know.

The good shepherd is literally, the savior of the sheep. Without him, they are dead mutton. They can't keep themselves healthy, fed, watered, or pastured, without his oversight. But a well-shepherded sheep is content, happy, and at peace. He thrives under the guarding staff of the good shepherd. When Jesus called himself the good shepherd, he fulfilled everything both David and Ezekiel wrote about. I love Christ's words in John 10:27-28, *"My sheep listen to my voice; I know them and they follow me. I give them eternal life and they shall never perish; no one can snatch them out of my hand."*

If we are sheep in the good shepherd's pasture then we know and listen to the voice of our good shepherd. We follow his voice, and he leads us into eternal life. Nothing can ever snatch us out of his hand! Oh, that is a powerful message for us to internalize. We are secure in the pasture of the good shepherd. Why? Because, his nature is to save and keep us. My security is not in a set of categorical syllogisms that make it impossible for me to be lost (as some theologies teach), but rather in the wonderful nature of my good shepherd. I am secure forever because I am his.

We are Living Stones being built into a Spiritual House

Several of the connections we have with God are repeated in more than one location of the Bible, but the one we will examine now is mentioned by Apostle Peter only once in 1 Peter 2:5 where we read, *"you also, like living stones, are being built into a spiritual house to be a holy priesthood, offering spiritual sacrifices acceptable to God through Jesus Christ."* We may not be drawn, at first glance, to the concept of stones, which seems kind of cold and impersonal. But notice that Peter teaches us that these stones are living. We're not talking about a pile of bricks lying around on the ground. This is an organized collection of living stones being built up together into a spiritual house. And like a multi-faceted gem, we catch a glint of another way God has wrapped us up into Himself.

Though God may save us as individuals, He doesn't let us stay that way. Instead, he builds us together into the church which is a spiritual house built to His glory. Peter changes the metaphor somewhat by talking about these living stones being a holy priesthood, offering up spiritual sacrifices to God through Jesus Christ. No inanimate brick could accomplish the task of offering up spiritual sacrifices. But it is obvious that Peter is reminding us that God not only places us in his family, He also builds us into the church which is a spiritual house built to God's glory.

A similar metaphor has Christ as the head while we are parts of the same body. In each word picture, we notice that we are interacting with each other like living stones in a building, and like organs in the body with Christ as head. The living stone metaphor is not complete until we read further in First Peter and notice that Jesus is the corner stone of the same building into which we are built together. He is the head of the body, and he is the foundational cornerstone of the building. We must understand that we cannot be built up into a spiritual house unless we are willing to be built up together as living stones mortared together into one building. Furthermore, we must interact with Christ as our chief cornerstone.

I've met a few Christians who were fine with their connection to Christ, but disinterested in connecting with others in the church. It is sad to see the way certain people fail to recognize the connection Christ has with the church. He is the head of the church, the cornerstone of the spiritual building, and the bridegroom of his bride, which is the church. Though some individuals may not be smitten with the church, Christ was never so devil-may-care about his connection to the church.

Christ loved the church so much he died for her, and he will some day present her to himself as a radiant bride without spot or wrinkle (Ephesians 5:25-27). The living stones metaphor not only connects us to God, but also interconnects us to each other as parts of a spiritual house. We must learn to see both connections or else we miss the whole point.

A Plethora of Metaphorical connections

Between them all, Apostles Paul, Peter and John did a masterful job of wrapping us up in God. They paint the following word pictures. We notice that Christians are seen as:

- Ambassadors, 2 Corinthians 5:20
- Believers, 2 Timothy 4:12
- Branches, John 15:5
- Aliens and Exiles (in relationship to the world), 1 Peter 2:11
- The bride of Christ, Revelation 19:7

And finally Paul gives 6 rapid fire metaphors in 2 Timothy 2 describing each Christian as:

- A soldier, vs. 4

- An athlete, vs. 5
- A farmer, vs. 6
- A workman, vs. 15
- A consecrated vessel, vs. 20-21
- A servant, vs. 24

Though so much more could be presented to make the case for our connections to God, we have a more than adequate picture of the ways God has lovingly picked us up and enfolded us within Himself. Like the nesting dolls from Russia, we have been placed so securely within God's loving provision and watch care that we have no need to worry about somehow being shaken out of our secure position in Him. This is a position we have inherited and it is secure in every way. Consider Peter's great Doxology about our inheritance: I Peter 1:3-5, *"Praise be to the God and Father of our Lord Jesus Christ! In his great mercy he has given us new birth into a living hope through the resurrection of Jesus Christ from the dead, and into an inheritance that can never perish, spoil or fade – kept in heaven for you, who through faith are shielded by God's power until the coming of the salvation that is ready to be revealed in the last time."*

Questions to Consider:

1. Looking at the various ways God has related us to himself, which of these connections is most meaningful to you?
2. From Colossians 3:1-3, what does it mean to be "hidden with Christ in God"?
3. When you think of being a child of God, what are you most thankful for in that context?
4. When you hear that Christians are saints, are you more inclined to see yourself as a saint or as a "wretch like me" (lyrics to Amazing Grace)?
5. When Peter refers to Christians as "living stones being built into a spiritual house" (1 Peter 2:5) what does that word picture tell you about yourself?
6. Which word picture about our connection with God brings the most joy to you as a Christian?
7. What is the connection between spiritual adoption and spiritual begetting? Why are both important? (Romans 8:15, John 1:12-13, 1 Peter 1:23)
8. Why is it important that the scriptures refer to Christians as Saints? (2 Thessalonians 1:10)
9. Why did Jesus refer to his followers as sheep, and why is it important for Jesus to be our good shepherd? (John 10:27-28)
10. Why does the Bible use so many different metaphors to describe our relationship with God? Which one is most meaningful to you?

Chapter 3: The Covenant Origin of Our Inheritance

Key Scripture: Hebrews 9:15-17, *"For this reason Christ is the mediator of a new covenant, that those who are called may receive the promised eternal inheritance—now that he has died as a ransom to set them free from the sins committed under the first covenant. In the case of a will, it is necessary to prove the death of the one who made it because a will is in force only when somebody has died; it never takes effect while the one who made it is living."*

Patrick Henry was one of the well known founders of our nation. Perhaps his most memorable moment was a speech where he pronounced these famous words. "Give me Liberty or give me Death!" Another, not so well known moment in Mr. Henry's life was the writing of his last will and testament before his death. His Last Will & Testament was filed in the Brookneal County courthouse in Virginia. You read his will and you'll see that he bequeathed everything to his children, just as most people do. But the last paragraph in his will is especially interesting. He wrote, "I have now given everything I own to my children. There is one more thing I wish I could give them and that is Christ. Because if they have everything I gave them and don't have Christ, they have nothing."

The most commonly recognized way for a person to inherit something from another person is through instructions written in a last will and testament. The inheritance is bestowed only after the death of the testator. Our inheritance from God is no different, except that God, the writer of the will, is eternal and can never die. Therefore, our inheritance depends on promises made by one who continues to live after the will and testament is written. In scripture we find a series of covenants God made with Adam, Noah, Abraham, Moses, David, and others who chose to enter into relationship with Him. These Old Testament covenants are precursors to our full inheritance as Christians.

A study of the covenants underscores the fact that not all covenants are alike. Some of the covenants were conditional in nature. Their validity depended on one or both parties keeping their end of the covenant. For example, the covenant which gave us the Mosaic Law, was a conditional covenant. It required the obedience of the people who lived under its tenants. Consequences were imposed on people who disobeyed. This covenant was full of "if-then" statements. In essence it said, "If you obey me, then I will bless you; if you disobey me, then I will curse you." Because it was conditional, it was also temporary. In fact, all conditional covenants are temporary in nature.

The Abrahamic Covenant

The story of Abraham is remarkable in many ways. Imagine leaving a place where you are settled and comfortable (Ur), to spend the remainder of your life living in tents as a nomad. Imagine doing this solely because a previously unknown deity promised to take you someplace he would show you later. Imagine being part of a childless couple getting up in age and yet having an ironic name that means "Father of Many" (Abram). Imagine God increasing the irony by changing your name to Abraham, which means "Father of a Multitude."

Imagine waiting until you and your spouse are far past the age of childbearing. Imagine living as a stranger in a strange land with the promise that, someday in the distant future, your descendants would actually possess the land. Every part of Abraham's adventure required faith, and Abraham proved himself to be a man of exemplary faith.

Genesis 15:6 tells us that Abraham believed God's covenant promises, and his faith was credited to him as righteousness. Of all the Old Testament covenants, the covenant between God and Abraham could be considered the most pivotal. The promises of this covenant included two physical elements and a third element which was spiritual in nature. Abraham was promised a tract of land, numerous descendants, and a comprehensive blessing. This covenant was eternal and irrevocable.

If a covenant is to be permanent, it cannot be conditional. God's covenant with Abraham (Genesis 12:1-3, 15:1-20) was an unconditional covenant. Therefore, the Abrahamic covenant is still in force today. In fact, our inheritance in Christ is based on God's covenant with Abraham. We receive the part of the covenant where God promised, "...*and all peoples on earth will be blessed through you*" (Genesis 12:3). We are covered by this promise in a general, all-inclusive sense ("all peoples"), and we are also covered because, as members of God's family, we are heirs to all that was promised to Abraham and his descendants. By faith we are children of Abraham and heirs to all that was promised to him (Romans 4:16, Galatians 3:6-14).

The unconditional quality of the Abrahamic covenant ensures that we cannot break the covenant through our own misdeeds. If we were living under the Levitical covenant we would be in constant danger of breaking some part of the law, and thereby falling under the curses of the law. Praise God, for he has provided a more permanent covenant than that which was given to Moses. The covenant under which we live came before the Mosaic Law, and will remain in force forever.

Believers enjoy all the promises given to Abraham's descendants without having to endure the restrictive commands of the Levitical system. I mention this here because there have always been false teachers who try to tie us back into the Levitical Law system. The letter to the Galatians warns against legalism that enslaves Christians to the Levitical Law. As Christians, we live under a better and more permanent covenant than that which was given at Mt. Horeb. Christ has set us free from the impossible conditions of the law. By faith, we inherit an unconditional and eternal covenant.

The Covenant ratified by Christ's death

An inheritance is bestowed only after a death. However, our covenant is from an eternal God who cannot die. Therefore, our God willingly put on flesh (John 1:14) and submitted to death as a human. Then he rose again as executor of our glorious inheritance. *"For this reason Christ is the mediator of a new covenant, that those who are called may receive the promised eternal inheritance—now that he has died as a ransom to set them free from the sins committed under the first covenant. In the case of a will, it is necessary to prove the death of the one who made it, because a will is in force only when somebody has died; it never takes effect while the one who made it is living."* (Hebrews 9: 15-17)

By Christ's death on the cross, he ratified for us a new and better testament. In fact, Paul tells us that when Christ was crucified, the Levitical law died with him. *"... having canceled the written code, with its regulations, that was against us and that stood opposed to us; he took it away, nailing it to the cross* (Colossians 2:14).

When Christ died on the cross, we died with him. In so doing, we were released from a legal, but miserable marriage to the law. Old Husband Law was a harsh and demanding marriage partner, never satisfied with his bride. Because we died with Christ, we are legally released from that marriage, and become, instead, the bride of Christ.

We have inherited an eternal covenant that is unconditional and flowing over with grace! This new covenant was ratified by death three times over. As testator of the will, Jesus Christ died and rose again. The law covenant itself was put to death on the cross with Christ. By faith, we also have died and we are resurrected with Christ.

Marriage to a New Law

The marriage analogy that Paul gives in Romans is rich with meaning. Romans 7:1-14 describes the Levitical Law as a demanding husband. I picture the finicky and fussy husband giving the "white glove treatment" to every surface in the house. He reaches up to run his gloved fingers across the top of the refrigerator. Then he shows his hapless wife the grime he has uncovered. Never mind that she is too short to reach that surface without a ladder. By the time Husband Law has finished revealing the many unclean surfaces, his wife is demoralized. Perfect Law has requirements that his all-too-human wife can never satisfy.

Of course, she could escape this miserable marriage and find a better husband if Husband Law ever died. Unfortunately for her, Perfect Law is in perfect health. The only hope left to the wife is if she, herself, could die and then come back to life as a new person. The marriage bond to the old husband would then be broken and she would be free to marry somebody else (Romans 7:4-6). This is precisely what Jesus Christ has provided for us.

Romans chapter 8 shouts the theme of our new status before God. *"Therefore there is now no condemnation for those who are in Christ Jesus"* (Romans 8:1). We've been set free from fussy, finicky Husband Law, and his constant condemnation. Even better, we now have a new husband. *"For the law of the Spirit of life in Christ Jesus has set us free from the law of sin and death"* (Romans 8:2). We have been set free from one law and we are now married to another law. We have died to the law of sin and death and have been reborn under a new law: *"the law of the Spirit of life in Christ Jesus."* This new law is not a law of condemnation, but a law of life in the Holy Spirit.

Old Husband Law focused on our inadequacies. Our new husband loves us with unconditional love. He never demands anything from us that he won't also perform within us. His law of the Spirit gives us new life. We find that when our minds are set on the Spirit we no longer fulfill the lusts of the flesh (Romans 8:4-11). Our life has been transformed from miserable to miraculous, for the presence of the Holy Spirit enables us to satisfy every requirement of our new and gracious husband.

In the same way that physical inheritance comes from a written promise contained in a Last Will and Testament, our spiritual inheritance started out as a promise from God himself. That promise given to Abraham so long ago is still in force today. It is God's promise that paved the way for all that we have inherited. We can look back to that promise and see ourselves receiving a blessing as heirs. What a rich heritage we have because God always keeps his promises!

Questions to Consider:

1. Have you ever inherited anything from someone who has died? Were you present to hear the reading of the will?

2. What does it mean to be a participant in the Abrahamic Covenant even though we may not be part of the Jewish race? (Romans 4:16, Galatians 3:6-14)

3. Even though the Levitical Law cannot die, how are we able to escape from the penalties of breaking that law? (Romans 7:1-6)

4. What did Christ do to ratify his new covenant with us? (Hebrews 9:15-17

5. If we are Christians, what law are we now living under, and what is the result of living under that law? (Romans 8:1-2)

6. How does a promise made to Abraham so long ago affect us today? What part of that promise was meant for us? (Genesis 12:3)

7. Why did Apostle Paul write that the Law was nailed to the cross, and what is significant about that fact in relation to us. (Colossians 2:14)

8. How does the spirit of life in Christ Jesus set us free from the law of sin and death? (Romans 8:2)

9. What are we enabled to do so that we no longer fulfill the lusts of the flesh? (Romans 8:4-11)

Chapter 4: The Indwelling Presence of the Holy Spirit

Key Verses: Ephesians 1:13-14, *"And you also were included in Christ when you heard the word of truth, the gospel of your salvation. Having believed, you were marked in him with a seal, the promised Holy Spirit, who is a deposit guaranteeing our inheritance until the redemption of those who are God's possession – to the praise of his glory."*

The Old Covenant Presence of God

When we look into the Covenant God made with Moses in the wilderness, we notice his desire to be close to the people he saved from Egyptian slavery. He instructed Moses to have the people construct for him a tabernacle which would be placed in the middle of the encampment of Israel (Exodus 25-30).

This special tent of meeting and the enclosure that surrounded it was to become the place where God's presence dwelled among the people. In fact, during the wilderness wanderings the people knew of God's nearness by sight for they saw a pillar of cloud by day and a pillar of fire by night above the holy place in the tent (Exodus 13:20-22). Whenever it was time for Israel to move to another location the pillar would rise and begin to move. This was the signal for Israel to strike all the tents and prepare to move with God's presence.

The 40 years of wilderness wanderings and living in tents as a nomadic people was replaced by living in houses as a settled people when Joshua and Caleb led Israel into the promised land of Canaan. Still, for hundreds of years, God's presence dwelled in the Tabernacle even though the pillar of cloud and fire was no longer resting over the tent as it had during the 40 years of wandering. Eventually Solomon, the son of King David, was given the task of building a temple to God's glory. The temple in Jerusalem replaced the Tabernacle as the place for God's presence to reside.

God commanded three sets of feasts to be celebrated in Israel every year, and for the men of Israel to come to Jerusalem to the holy place where God dwelled to offer sacrifices and to celebrate the barley, wheat, and wine harvests with the Feast of unleavened bread, Passover, First-fruits, Feast of Weeks, Feast of Trumpets, Day of Atonement, and Feast of Booths (Exodus 23:14-17, Leviticus 23).

All of this was evidence of God's desire to be close to his people and to celebrate the connection between God and His covenant people on a regular basis. Though it was meaningful for God to interact with his people in this way, the history of the Old Testament reveals repeatedly that his covenant people strayed away from that connection in their hearts. They would continue to bring the sacrifices, but without passion in their hearts for God.

In fact, the Prophet Isaiah begins his letter to Israel with an emotional lament from Jehovah where he reveals his displeasure with Israel's animal sacrifices. *"The multitude of your sacrifices – what are they to me" says the Lord. "I have more than enough of burnt offerings, or rams and the fat of fattened animals; I have no pleasure in the blood of bulls and lambs and goats. When you come to meet with me, who has asked this of you, this trampling of my courts? Stop bringing meaningless offerings! Your incense is detestable to me. New Moons, Sabbaths, and convocations – I cannot bear your evil assemblies. Your new moon festivals and your appointed feasts my soul hates. They have become a burden to me; I am weary of bearing them. When you spread out your hands in prayer, I will hide my eyes from you; even if you offer many prayers I will not listen. Your hands are full of blood; wash and make yourselves clean. Take your evil deeds out of my sight! ... Isaiah 1:11-16*

It is bad enough when people get sick of going to church (so to speak) but so much worse when God is the one who has had his fill of it. The problem was pretense and symbolism over substance. The people drew near to God with their lips while their hearts were far away from him (Isaiah 29:13). It became obvious that dwelling in close proximity to the covenant people was not enough. For God to allow his presence to reside in a tent or temple and have people visit that place now and then was not sufficient for either God or his people. There needed to be something better than this, and God communicated what that better thing would be. Through the prophets, God began to outline a new covenant he would make with his people. Under this new covenant, God would no longer reside in tents or temples. Instead he would take up residence in men's hearts.

Consider this promise found in Jeremiah 31:33-34: *"This is the covenant I will make with the house of Israel after that time," declares the Lord. "I will put my law in their minds and write it on their hearts. I will be their God, and they will be my people. No longer will a man teach his neighbor, or a man his brother, saying, 'Know the Lord,' because they will all know me, from the least of them to the greatest," declares the Lord. "For I will forgive their wickedness and will remember their sins no more."*

The New Covenant Ministry of the Holy Spirit

Throughout the Old Testament the Holy Spirit would make periodic appearances, but the presence of the Spirit was always temporary in duration. During Jesus' ministry on earth, the presence of the Holy Spirit was upon Jesus as evidenced at his baptism when the Holy Spirit came upon him visibly in the form of a dove (Matthew 3:16-17, Mark 1:9-11,Luke 3:21-22).

At the Last Supper, Jesus explained to his men about the coming ministry of the Holy Spirit. He said to them, *"When the Counselor comes, whom I will send to you from the Father, the Spirit of Truth who goes out from the Father, he will testify about me… It is for your good that I am going away. Unless I go away, the Counselor will not come to you; but if I go, I will send him to you…" (John 15:26, 16:7)*

After Jesus resurrection from the dead, he made numerous appearances to his disciples and other believers. It was during this forty day period between his resurrection and his ascension that he told his men to wait for the Holy Spirit to come upon them (Acts 1:4-5). Ten days after Jesus' ascension, the Holy Spirit fell with power on the day of Pentecost and the church was born (Acts 2). This marked the time of fulfillment of the prophecy in Jeremiah 31:33-34.

What we have come to call the church age, is the time when God's laws are written in men's hearts and God himself dwells in the form of the Holy Spirit with the spirits of believers all over the world. This also marks the end of any need for further animal sacrifices, the Levitical priesthood, or for a tabernacle or temple. The finished work of Christ on the cross, and the presence of the Holy Spirit with those Christ has redeemed makes for a remarkably new and vastly superior era than the 1,500 year period of the Levitical law. The book of Hebrews in the New Testament is an excellent treatise on all the ways the New Covenant is better than the Old Covenant. One of the improvements is the ministry of the indwelling presence of the Holy Spirit in the believer.

So what does the Holy Spirit's presence do in the believer? Consider the ministries the scriptures enumerate for us:

- **Counselor/comforter**: The Greek word (paracletos) literally means "to come along beside". When Jesus introduced the Holy Spirit to his men at the last supper he used that name to describe the one he would send back to them after he left (John 14:26). Today a large portion of our population uses the services of counselors because of all the emotional turmoil and stress people undergo in the course of life. The Holy Spirit is called a counselor/comforter because that is a major part of his ministry within us. We can literally seek advice and comfort from the divine presence living in our bodies.

- **Teacher**: After calling the Holy Spirit "the counselor", Jesus went on to tell his men that the Spirit would teach them all things and bring to remembrance all that he had told them (John 14:26). Jesus also called the Holy Spirit the "Spirit of truth", which lets us know that the Spirit teaches us God's truth. Apostle Paul echoed that concept in I Cor. 2:13 explaining that the Spirit teaches, not in human wisdom, but expressing spiritual truths in spiritual words. The nature of this ministry implies communication from the Holy Spirit to the person in whom He dwells, which brings up the question of how that may be done. Some Christians testify that the Spirit speaks to them using words they can understand. Others affirm more the process of urging or nudging attributed to the Spirit. I suspect that the process of teaching from the Holy Spirit is unique with each believer.

- **Guide**: On one of his missionary journeys, Apostle Paul sought guidance from the Holy Spirit as to which way to go and which group of people to evangelize. Acts 16:6-7 records the Spirit forbidding them to go to Asia or Bithynia. Then the next night Paul had a dream where a man from Macedonia called him to come over and help them. The Spirit is able to reveal God's will and His plan for us if we are in tune with his attempts to communicate with us. Because the Holy Spirit is our guide, we are commanded to "walk by the Spirit" and promised that if we do this we will not fulfill the lust of the flesh (Galatians 5:16, 25).

- **Witness**: Jesus explained to his men that the Holy Spirit, which came from the Father would bear witness of him (John 15:26). The Spirit is able to give testimony concerning Christ. In fact, Jesus said that the Spirit always pointed to Jesus and not to Himself. (John 16:13-15)

- **Helper**: The Holy Spirit can help the Christian to overcome sin in his life because it is by the Spirit that we are enabled to put to death the deeds of the body (Romans 8:12-13). (There will be more about this overcoming power in chapter 5.)

- **Intercessor**: At times, we are unable to express ourselves adequately in prayer. This is when the Holy Spirit takes over and prays to the Father for us. How reassuring to know, that God has planted an intercessor within us, who intercedes for us constantly. The Father and the Spirit are in constant connection in our behalf (Romans 8:26).

- **Seal of Ownership**: When God saved and regenerated us, the Holy Spirit was placed within us as a seal of ownership. We are God's unique possession, and the Spirit's presence within us is the proof of that blessed condition. In fact the Holy Spirit is called the down-payment ("earnest", KJV) of our inheritance (Ephesians 1:13-14; 4:30). Some may wonder how God will know that we belong to him when we arrive in heaven. The presence of the Spirit within us is the official seal of our son-ship in God's family (Romans 8:9-11, 16).

Our Responsibilities in light of the Spirit's Presence

How amazing it is for God to take up residence inside us. Surely you must know that such an honor carries certain responsibilities with it. God is not interested in taking up residence in any old dwelling. He is pleased to be planted in the body of the believer, but his presence demands certain accommodations. If we do the things the scriptures advise for us, our interactions with the Spirit will be smooth and satisfying for both of us:

- **Walk in the Spirit**: I mentioned this earlier regarding the Spirit as our guide, but restate it here to show that the Holy Spirit can only guide us if we are willing to be guided, and that presupposes that we are walking beside our guide (Galatians 5:16, 25). Jesus taught his men a corollary to this when he spoke about abiding in the vine (John 15). Walking in the Spirit and abiding in the vine are twin truths. We cannot run ahead or lag behind the Spirit and be led by him. Consider the fascinating metaphor in Psalm 32:9 which illustrates this principle, *"Do not be like the horse or the mule, which have no understanding but must be controlled by bit and bridle or they will not come to you.* The Holy Spirit cannot guide or teach anyone who is a truant from his class room.

- **Don't grieve the Spirit**: This command is found in Ephesians 4:30. Chapter 4 of Ephesians gives instructions for how to walk worthy of the calling we have received (Ephesians 4:1). Among the admonitions given, we are advised not to grieve the Holy Spirit in whom we were sealed for the day of redemption. The implication of this admonition is that the resident Holy Spirit is a divine person; not just an ethereal force. Like Jesus Christ, the Holy Spirit, who Paul calls, "Christ in you, the hope of glory" (Colossians 1:27) is a presence with a mind, will, and emotions. You would naturally be respectful and polite to a house guest, so why treat the indwelling Spirit of Christ with any worse manners than you would extend to another human? The admonition not to grieve the Holy Spirit implies that we can cause him grief by our behavior.

- **Don't quench the Spirit**: 1 Thessalonians 5:19 provides the admonition not to quench the Spirit. This admonition may be somewhat related to the teaching about not grieving the Spirit, but perhaps this may be one of greater intensity. To grieve the Spirit implies placing him in an emotional state where he cries out in your behalf to the Father. The possibility of quenching the Spirit implies making his work within you to become completely ineffective. For all the good he is able to accomplish within you, it would be like he wasn't even there. God is often represented in the Old Testament as a fire (Deuteronomy 4:24: 9:3), so quenching the Spirit would be like pouring water on a fire. If God is going to take up residence within us, we want him to be able to do whatever he wishes to accomplish his purpose within us. Therefore, we do not wish to grieve or quench the Spirit.

- **Be filled with the Spirit**: This admonition is found several places (Ephesians 5:18; Acts 4:32; 6:3; 13:52). The ultimate objective of the Christian walk is total submission to the leading of the Spirit so that we move in perfect harmony with his direction. This is not to imply that the Holy Spirit comes in pints, quarts, and gallons like some liquid we could drink to the full, but rather to suggest that the Spirit might have such voluntary control over our spirit that we are able to say like Christ did, that he always did whatever he saw his Father doing (John 8:28-29). In our Spiritual growth we develop more of the mind of Christ, and have a greater desire to do God's will. By seeing Christ's glory as it is we are transformed from one degree of glory to the next by the Spirit (2 Corinthians 3:18). Spirit filling is not merely an option for the Christian. We are tempted to assume that spirit filling is for ministers and missionaries and others who are more "full time" in ministry. But looking into the selection of deacons to serve tables in Acts 6:3 we notice that the Apostles instructed the selection of men who were "full of the Spirit and wisdom". Spirit filling is for normal every day Christians. It comes along with growing to maturity. The Christians who walk daily in the Spirit and follow after the

Spirit in obedience will find themselves filling up with the presence and power of the Spirit. This is the goal of the daily Christian walk.

Throughout the Bible, the story of God's dealings with mankind revealed his desire to develop a close and personal relationship with his creation. It was not enough to merely be among the people, which was the situation when God took up residence in the Holy of Holies in the Tabernacle and later in the Temple. It was not enough to write his laws on stone tablets or have men write them on scrolls. His desire was to take up residence in the hearts of the humans he created and to make their bodies his temple.

With the coming of the Holy Spirit on the day of Pentecost, this change was accomplished. Today, in this present day we sometimes call the church age, we need to realize that what God wanted most, has been accomplished. He wanted to dwell in the hearts of men and women who call Him their God. Today God resides within us in the form of the Holy Spirit. Therefore, we need no human mediators to bring God closer to us, or to usher us into His presence. This has all been accomplished through the finished work of Christ and the present work of the Holy Spirit within us.

We have inherited the most excellent way of communication with God through his Spirit's presence in our spirits. We can rejoice in this "new and living way" to come directly into God's presence (Hebrews 10:20).

Questions to Consider:

1. What is the main difference between the work of God in the Old Testament times and the way He works today (Jeremiah 31:31-34)?

2. Of all the work the Holy Spirit can do in the life of the Christian, which of His many abilities is most helpful and needed in your life?

3. In what way does the Holy Spirit usually communicate with you?

4. Looking at our responsibilities in light of the Holy Spirit's presence within us, which of the four mentioned is the most difficult for you to do consistently?

5. What is your biggest road block to closer fellowship with God?

6. Jesus called the Holy Spirit the Paraclete (counselor/comforter) when he told his men about the coming ministry of the Spirit after he would leave the earth. Why do we need such a counselor/comforter in our lives today? (John 14:26)

7. What does it mean for the Holy Spirit to "seal" the Christian? (Romans 8:9-11,16)

8. How do we know when we are walking in the Spirit? (Galatians 5:16, 25)

9. What is the difference between grieving and quenching the Holy Spirit? Which is worse? (Ephesians 4:30, 1 Thessalonians 5:19)

10. What does it mean to be filled with the Spirit? How do you know if you are? (Ephesians 5:18, Acts 4:32; 6:3; 13:52)

Chapter 5: The Power to Overcome

Key scripture: Revelation 21:7, *"He who overcomes will inherit all this, and I will be his God and he will be my son."*

We have a propensity as Christians to fall back on our humanity as an excuse for not making progress in our spiritual walk. We say things like, "I'm only human," or "Can't teach an old dog new tricks." We are fond of slogans like, "Not perfect; just forgiven," or "I'm just a sinner, saved by grace." Such sayings have the appearance of humility, but may indicate lack of spiritual understanding. Scripture does not label believers as sinners. On the contrary, we are "more than conquerors through Him who loved us" (Romans 8:37). We were not saved by Christ so we could hang on by our fingernails until he finally swoops in to rescue us by His return. As believers we have inherited the status of conquerors.

Because Jesus Christ lives in us we have inherited divine enabling that was not available to us prior to our new birth. One such enabling is the power to overcome. John the Apostle repeatedly mentioned this power to overcome in his gospel, his first epistle, and his apocalyptic revelation. Naturally, this power is primarily related to victory in the arena of sin. But to understand its workings we must first comprehend its origin.

Our power to overcome finds its source in the original overcomer, Jesus Christ. The Apostle John recounts the words Jesus spoke to his men on the night he was arrested. *"I have told you these things, so that in me you may have peace. In this world you will have trouble. But take heart! I have overcome the world"* (John 16:33). The word "overcome" is a translation of the Greek word "nike" which means victory. Most of us are familiar with the sports attire and equipment company, which adopted that Greek word as the name of their company. We are used to seeing the Nike "swish" logo on clothes, tennis shoes, golf balls, and other sporting goods.

Although John was the most prolific user of the word "nike," the Apostle Paul also used the term in a powerful way. In Romans 8 he wrote: *"No, in all these things we are more than conquerors through him who loved us"* (Romans 8:37). Paul took an already potent word "nike" and gave it an even more powerful prefix "huper". Put together, "huper nikomai" means super-victor or hyper-overcomer. Through Christ, we have received overwhelming victory over sin, the devil, and the world system. We may sometimes act like "under-goers" but our inherited destiny is to live as overcomers.

John has more to say about the overcomers in 1 John 5:4-5*: "For everyone born of God overcomes the world. This is the victory that has overcome the world, even our faith. Who is it that overcomes the world? Only he who believes, that Jesus is the Son of God."* Notice that to believe is to overcome. John teaches that everyone born of God overcomes the world. This is a powerful principle to tuck inside our heads. Believers are not commanded to become overcomers. Believers already *are* overcomers! By virtue of belief in Jesus they have overcome the world.

This principle is valid whether we choose to live by it or not. We may not always appropriate this truth into our lives. Our experience of this truth depends on spiritual enlightenment and our own volition. When we see our true identity in Christ, and when we choose to live by that faith, we will experience the overcoming power of Christ himself in our daily lives.

John explains this process in 1 John 4:4, *"You, dear children, are from God and have overcome them, because the one who is in you is greater than the one who is in the world."* Once again, we can't help but notice that overcoming power is wrapped up in Christ himself. Overcoming is a by-product of letting the original overcomer live his life within us. We ourselves, are easily defeated by sin, the Devil, and the world system. He is not. Therefore, overcoming is not a matter of trying harder, but of trusting more. Let us rest in his presence so that his power can work within us.

Those who are in Christ Jesus have the privilege of living exchanged lives. Paul described the exchanged life in Galatians 2:20: "I live; yet not I, but Christ lives in me: and the life which I now live in the flesh I live by the faith of the Son of God, who loved me, and gave himself for me" (KJV).

Friends, God did not plant the Holy Spirit within us for him to just sit there doing nothing inside us. In fact, I suspect that some of us have bound and gagged the Spirit within us lest he do anything beyond our control. We are so fearful of what he might do in us, that we keep him stifled (quenched and grieved, see chapter 4) so that nothing unexpected happens in our lives, then, we wonder why we live frustrated and disappointing lives as Christians.

The Holy Spirit is described as "Christ in you, the hope of glory" (Colossians 1:27). We weren't meant to do everything on our own power, while Christ sits idly by, watching passively. The real problem is that we don't trust Him. Let's be honest here. If we did trust Him, then we would enter into an adventure where we dwell with Christ, both living in the same body, and doing ministry together as a team. Don't you suppose that is what "abiding in Christ" (John 15) is all about? (You must realize that when a preacher writes a book, he will occasionally lapse into preaching, even on the page.)

Some may naturally assume that overcoming is a quality eventually achieved over time by those who become fully mature. But when John writes his letter to the church he is talking to various groups at differing levels of maturity. Notice what he has to say to the little children, to the young men, and to the fathers: "…I write to you, dear children, because you have known the Father. I write to you, fathers, because you have known him who is from the beginning. I write to you, young men, because you are strong, and the word of God lives in you, and you have overcome the evil one" (I John 2:13b-14). That passage reveals that believers who have not reached full maturity are able to be strong, with the word of God living in them, and having overcome the evil one.

First John 4:4 shows why even young believers are already overcomers. "You, dear children, are from God and have overcome them, because the one who is in you is greater than the one who is in the world." The ability to overcome rests squarely upon Christ who is the original overcomer (John 16:33). We are overcomers, not because of anything we have attained, but because Christ is present in our lives (I John 5:4-5).

Please divest yourself of the notion that you cannot be an overcomer until you achieve full maturity as a believer. Just as we trust in Christ alone for salvation, so we must trust Christ alone for the power to overcome sin. If you can overcome by virtue of your own willpower and determination, then who needs Christ for anything? Do it all yourself! See how far you get on your own power. Chances are, you will try…and fail … and then come back to an understanding of how necessary Christ is for any positive outcome. Jesus told his men at the last Supper, "Apart from me, you can do nothing" (John 15:5b).

The Apostle John wrote something else about overcoming that helps us understand the source of overcoming power. In Revelation 12:11 John tells about overcoming the accuser of the brethren and states how this will be accomplished: "They overcame him by the blood of the Lamb and by the word of their testimony; they did not love their lives so much as to shrink from death." Once again, we notice how Christ himself fits into this picture. It is the blood of the Lamb that provides overcoming power. And along with that power comes a corresponding testimony of those who were willing to even die if necessary. The power is from Christ. The result of that power, applied to a believer, is the ability to remain faithful even unto death.

Rewards to the Overcomers

In Revelation chapters 2 and 3, Jesus writes seven letters to second-generation churches in Asia. In each letter he has a personal message of encouragement, and sometimes admonition for the congregation. The most fascinating part of this section of Revelation is the fact that each letter contains a special message to "him who overcomes." In every instance, Christ himself bestows specific rewards to the overcomers.

- *…To him who overcomes, I will give the right to eat from the tree of life, which is in the paradise of God* (Revelation 2:7). Two gifts are given here, the right to eat from the tree of life, and the implied entrance into heaven. Overcomers will eat freely from the same tree that was removed from the Garden of Eden after the fall of Adam and Eve (Genesis 3:22-24). We know from Revelation 22:2 that the tree of life will be on both sides of the River of Life in Heaven, and that it will produce 12 crops of fruit, one each month. Considering that I enjoy eating food so much, it is reassuring to know that food is available in heaven. This reward tells us something about the joy and fulfillment of paradise.

- *Be faithful, even to the point of death, and I will give you the crown of life...He who overcomes will not be hurt at all by the second death* (Revelation 2:10-11). Two gifts are mentioned here. The first is a Crown of Life given to anyone who is faithful even to the point of death. The crown mentioned here is a "stephanos" or victor's crown. This crown signifies victory and joy, completion, special recognition as an honored one, and free access to the presence of God. This could be called a martyr's crown, and it makes the second gift even more meaningful. Anyone willing to endure persecution to the point of death has nothing to fear from the second death, for he will bypass it entirely. The second death refers to those who will be condemned to the lake of fire (Revelation 20:14, 21:8). It is reassuring for Jesus to state plainly that those who are raised to new life after earthly death will never again experience death.

- *To him who overcomes, I will give some of the hidden manna. I will also give him a white stone with a new name written on it, known only to him who receives it* (Revelation 2:17). Here we see that three gifts are mentioned. The first is the manna that was hidden in the Ark of the Covenant beneath the mercy seat. It was evidence of God's daily provision during the 40 years of wandering, sometimes referred to as bread of heaven. This gives evidence that things exist in heaven which have disappeared from the earth. This manna is a symbol of Jehovah Jireh, God who is our provision. The white stone, which is the second reward, has several possible meanings. The stone may refer to God's declaration of innocence or acquittal. In the justice system of that day, a black stone would have meant condemnation or disapproval. The stone may indicate God's selection of the overcomer as his favored possession. It could be a ticket for entrance into the heavenly places, or a symbol of retirement with honor. The third reward is the new name which is written on the stone. This name, known only between Christ and the recipient, shows the privileged relationship between the individual believer and Jesus. During his ministry on earth Jesus was inclined to give his men new names, so the idea of giving each overcomer a new name shows his personal interest in every believer.

- *...To him who overcomes and does my will to the end, I will give authority over the nations— 'He will rule them with an iron scepter; he will dash them to pieces like pottery'— just as I have received authority from my Father. I will also give him the morning star* (Revelation 2:26-28). Again, we notice two gifts, the first of which is authority to rule beside Jesus, perhaps during the millennial reign of Christ. This would imply that we will not spend our days in heaven in idleness, but will be involved in ministry for our Lord. The idea of ruling with Christ is also mentioned in 2 Timothy 2:12, *"If we endure, we will also reign with him."* The second reward, the Morning Star, is a title mentioned in Isaiah 14:12. Some assume this had been Lucifer's title before his rebellion and fall. At any rate, it seems most likely that this title, along with others, will be given to the resurrected "root and offspring of David" (Revelation 22:16). If overcomers are given the morning star, it seems to signify their possession of Jesus in all his glory.

- *"He who overcomes will, like them, be dressed in white. I will never blot out his name from the Book of Life, but will acknowledge his name before my Father and his angels* (Revelation 3:5). Under the Levitical Law white garments were worn by priests involved in tabernacle or temple duties. Like the white stone mentioned earlier, white garments indicate righteousness and acceptance. The book of Revelation presents Jesus returning to earth as a mighty warrior, accompanied by his mighty armies, all wearing white garments (Revelation 19:14). We are told that the bride of Christ will wear white garments representing the righteousness of the saints (Revelation 19:8). Those wearing these white garments will never have their names blotted out of the Book of Life, but will be acknowledged before the Father in heaven. Blotting out a name from a book implies that it was there originally. Some scholars hold to the idea that all people's names are written in the Book of Life, and that their names remain or are removed depending on what they do with Jesus Christ. It also explains why the Book of Life is called the Lamb's book of Life in Revelation 21:27. *"Nothing impure will ever enter it (heaven), nor will anyone who does what is shameful or deceitful, but only those whose names are written in the Lamb's Book of Life."*

- *Him who overcomes I will make a pillar in the temple of my God. Never again will he leave it. I will write on him the name of my God and the name of the city of my God, the new Jerusalem, which is coming down out of heaven from my God; and I will also write on him my new name* (Revelation 3:12). When John wrote to the church in Philadelphia, he wrote to people who were familiar with the terror of earthquakes. They knew what it was like to be in a building and have to leave it suddenly when they felt tremors in the earth. They knew the danger of being crushed by a collapsing building. They knew the importance of pillars. These Christians were undergoing persecution which often meant being dragged out of the worship house to be tortured or killed. For them, the promise of being a permanent pillar in God's temple would have great appeal. Historically, a pillar would sometimes be erected to honor a noble person who had died. On that pillar would be his name and the name of his father. The pillar signifies lasting honor. Nothing could possibly be more permanent than a pillar in the temple of heaven. God's name on that pillar signifies ownership. He will put his mark on his own. The New Jerusalem signifies heavenly citizenship, and the new name to which Jesus refers is a new title He will receive in Heaven. That new title will be written on our pillars. No one knows that title yet, but when that title is given to Jesus, it will also be written on us. We can feel secure of a permanent and noble position in God's house.

- *To him who overcomes, I will give the right to sit with me on my throne, just as I overcame and sat down with my Father on his throne*

(Revelation 3:21). Here we notice a reiteration of Paul's declaration that we are seated with Christ in the heavenly realms (Ephesians 2:6). Christ himself invites us to sit with Him on His throne. Jesus, unlike many who hoard their power, is willing to share his position of authority with his followers. This emphasizes the close nature of our relatedness to God. We are his children and joint heirs with God's unique son, Jesus. We are invited to enter the throne room and sit on the throne with Christ. I assume that is one big throne, to hold so many believers!

- *He who overcomes will inherit all this, and I will be his God and he will be my son* (Revelation 21:7). All that has been promised to overcomers is reiterated in Revelation 21:7. It brings to mind the way a quiz show host recites every prize in a showcase and then says, "You will win all this if the price is right." In an immensely greater way, God reminds the overcomers, that everything he has promised, the whole package, is included in their inheritance. He then adds, "and I will be his God and he will be my son." This is much different than a quiz show host who hands out prizes and then walks away from the prize winner. God's relationship with his overcomers is close and permanent. He remains their God for eternity and claims them as sons.

Our inheritance as overcomers is greater than we could ever imagine. In fact, the magnitude of these rewards will astound us for eternity. No honors assembly could compare with the glory God will reveal to his own. No military medal or sports trophy could begin to measure up with what God has in store for his children. He has given us a brief outline of the inheritance he will one day bestow on those who overcome.

Until then, what do overcomers do? We do just what the name implies. We overcome. We endure. We exhibit staying power. We cling to Christ and abide in Him as He abides in us. We do His will day to day. We remain faithful even unto death. When the going gets tough, remember your inheritance: the tree of life, the crown of life, the hidden manna and white stone, the morning star, the white robe, your name in the book of life, the pillar in God's temple, and your place with Christ on his throne. *He who overcomes will inherit all this, and I will be his God and he will be my son (*Revelation 21:7). What more could we possibly want?

Questions to consider:

1. In terms of your daily Christian experience would you describe yourself as more of an "under-goer" or an overcomer?

2. In John 16:33 when Jesus told his men at the Last Supper, "In this world you will have trouble, but take heart, I have overcome the world." What message was he giving them to help them with what was soon to come, and what do his words say to us today?

3. According to 1 John 5:4-5 who are the people who have the ability to overcome the world and what is the association that makes it possible?

4. What level of Christian maturity is required to be an overcomer?

5. Of all the gifts available to overcomers which one excites you the most?

6. What is the problem in "worm" theology where a Christian views himself as a "sinner saved by grace"?

7. If we see ourselves as overcomers how will that help us in our Christian lives?

8. In First John 5:4-5 who are the overcomers?

9. What does it mean to remain "faithful unto death" and what is the reward for such faithfulness? (Revelation 2:10-11)

10. What is the significance of a white garment? (Revelation 3:5)

Chapter 6: God's Unique Relationship to Each of Us

Key Scriptures: Psalm 139:13-18, *"For you created my inmost being; you knit me together in my mother's womb. I praise you because I am fearfully and wonderfully made; your works are wonderful, I know that full well. My frame was not hidden from you when I was made in the secret place. When I was woven together in the depths of the earth, your eyes saw my unformed body. All the days ordained for me were written in your book before one of them came to be. How precious to me are your thoughts, O God! How vast is the sum of them! Were I to count them, they would outnumber the grains of sand. When I awake, I am still with you."*

God's activity in creation has revealed something to us about himself and his way with his creation. For example, I am told that, although they are all six-sided, every snow flake is unique. Photos have been taken and compared by computer analysis to reveal that no two flakes are identical twins. According to physicist Kenneth Libbrecht, author of <u>Ken Libbrecht's Field Guide to Snowflakes</u>, "It is indeed extremely unlikely that two complex snowflakes will look exactly alike. It's so extremely unlikely, in fact, that even if you looked at every one ever made you would not find any exact duplicates."

What is true of snowflakes is also true of fingerprints, the retinas of human eyes, human DNA, and a host of other things. In all these things God has shown his immeasurable creativity and attention to minute detail. In revealing our immense value to our Father God, Jesus Christ said the very hairs on our heads are numbered (Luke 12:37). God has created each of us to be a unique, one of a kind work of his artistry. In the same way that God has created each of us to be one of a kind persons, I believe that he has also chosen to interact with each of us in a unique way.

My wife, Susan, and I are parents of two unique daughters. I can testify that they have two very different personalities, and that we parented them in different ways corresponding to what we knew about their personalities. One of our girls was more compliant, and one was more strong-willed. One was more of a perfectionist than the other. All we had to do to one of them was speak, and she melted into a puddle of tears, while the other needed stronger disciplinary measures. I still remember the evening, years ago, when both girls were studying for tests.

Susan went into the bedroom of one daughter who was fretting over an upcoming test and in tears about being prepared adequately for it, even though she had studied for hours. Susan advised her she had done all she could do. She told her not to worry about it so much because "school is not that important!"

Susan then walked into the bedroom of the other daughter to hear her reading the study guide out loud. "Can you name the five major rivers in Texas?" She answered her own question, "No." Then she moved blithely on to the next question. I heard Susan telling her to put real effort into her studies because "school is very important!" How ironic to encourage one child to chill out, and then walk next door to advise the other daughter to work harder.

Why the variation? Each child has a unique personality and unique needs. One-size- fits-all parenting doesn't work because no two children are alike.

Our heavenly Father and creator surely knows us well enough to parent each of us as we need it individually. I believe that each of us has inherited a unique relationship with a heavenly Father who knows us intimately. He knows how to motivate us as only a loving Father could.

When God created us, he used a specialized recipe for each person, outlining our physical features, our personalities, our propensities, and the number of days we will populate this planet (Psalm 139:16). Having planned out the details of our lives, God is able to parent us and shape our lives in unique ways. I also contend that God's call to each of us for salvation and for ministry is also unique, and customized for our personal needs.

I say all of this to make a certain point concerning what I often observe in Christian teaching about salvation and call into ministry. A common Christian teaching assumes that everyone who is regenerated in Christ has lived a life apart from God where they were headed in an obviously wrong direction, and that God dramatically turned them around and saved them from an obviously debauched life. In fact, the common expectation about the Christian "testimony" involves a recitation of life "before Christ" when they were hell bound (perhaps a member of a renegade motorcycle gang for example), and then part two of the testimony where they were grabbed up and saved. This is followed by the "after conversion" part of the testimony where a compare and contrast is given between the before-life and the after-life. This type of testimony works best for people who come to Christ as adults.

But what about those of us who, as far back as we can remember, have loved God and wanted to serve him. We came to appreciate God's love in the same way we learned about our parent's love. We certainly grew in understanding and we developed a deeper connection to our Father in heaven, but we can't remember going through a time of direct rebellion against God. For us, it is difficult to come up with a dramatic conversion testimony. Sadly, there are those in certain theological circles who have concluded that people without a before-and-after conversion testimony might not have actually been saved. Conventional wisdom posits that the proof of the pudding in salvation is dramatic change from the "before life" to the "after life." No dramatic moment of change seems to imply there was no true regeneration.

The early Puritans were plagued with this problem after they crossed the Atlantic and set things up in the new colonies. They had a theology that demanded dramatic evidence of conversion. But the children of these Puritans weren't always able to produce the proper evidence of transformation (such as a proper amount of tears into crying towels on the front row). Eventually the Puritan leaders created a "halfway covenant" membership category for these inadequately converted children. Perhaps the problem was not in the inadequacies of the second generation of believers, as much as it was the rigidity of the forms into which well intentioned Puritans were trying to stuff their children.

Is it possible that the rigid thinking of well-intentioned Christian leaders places some believers in an unfortunate limbo made up of theologically fashioned hurdles? What about the non-tongue speaking Pentecostal; the backslidden Baptist; the non-sanctified Nazarene; the non-sacramental Catholic? Is God able to do anything with those who don't fit into all theological boxes at the right time? I propose that He can and He does.

Jehovah described Himself to Moses as the "God of Abraham, Isaac, and Jacob" (Exodus 3:6). A study of God's interactions with each of these Patriarchs reveals not only the different personalities of each of these men, but also of God's differing actions with each of them.

With Abraham, God gave a call to new beginnings, pioneering, exploring, meeting strangers, unknown destinations, and risky adventures. Abraham's call demanded a complete and dramatic change of direction.

God dealt with Isaac in a very different way. Isaac was not called to make the changes and take the risks that Abraham had to take. Isaac never even dug a new well, though he re-opened some of his father's wells. In fact, the story of Isaac's life was one of faithful reception of what God had already provided his father. Isaac's call was to stay home. He never even left home to look for a wife. Instead he accepted the choice of a servant who went out looking on his behalf.

When we look at the life of Jacob, Isaac's son, we notice a different kind of interaction with God. This time we observe a personality that lived up to his name, Jacob, "the usurper" or "the grabber". Jacob was one who attempted, through clever and sometimes deceitful actions, to manipulate things to his own favor. At one point we notice him actually wrestling with God (Genesis 32:22-32). At that point, God gave him a new name, "Israel," which means "one who contends with God and prevails". These men illustrate three different personalities, and three corresponding methods of interaction from God. God is not tied into a cookie cutter, one-size-fits-all means of interaction.

Jesus' parable of the prodigal son in Luke 15:11-32 was an excellent picture of the mind of the Loving Father to the wayward child. You may remember that the son came home, but was the first to admit he had no right to be there. The elder brother certainly agreed with the younger brother's assessment. But it was the Father who declared son-ship and full acceptance as the proper lot for the son. The son never earned it or deserved it, but the Father restored fellowship to his wayward boy. The Father had two sons, but he treated them differently according to life choices and personality, and, most important, according to the unique needs of each son (See chapter 13 for a more complete analysis of this parable).

Another example of specialized treatment is found in John 11 where Jesus and his disciples arrived in Bethany after the death of Lazarus. Notice the differing way Jesus interacted with Martha as compared to his interaction with her sister, Mary. With Martha, Jesus carried on a theological conversation about resurrection from the dead. But when Jesus came face to face with Mary, he responded on a purely emotional level. Jesus was moved to tears by her sorrow. Jesus' behavior matched the individual needs of each sister.

An individual's call to salvation is one way God is able to demonstrate his unique dealings with each of his children. This is not to assume that God would bypass anything concerning his provision for spiritual begetting and birthing. We know God will not do anything for anyone apart from Christ and his finished work on the cross. But in terms of God's way of interacting with each sinner, I believe His call to each sinner is custom designed.

The second unique calling of God is the call to service. Once again, there seems to be an expected scenario for the testimony of ministers about their calling into ministry. The one-size-fits-all approach would have every one of us mirroring the story of Jonah who had to be eaten by a great fish in order to be brought into conformity to his calling to preach to the wicked Ninevites. Is a call to ministry only valid if the potential minister starts out dead set against going into the ministry? Must each minister be dragged screaming and kicking against the "call" to preach? Is that the only litmus test for a genuine call to preach?

I once feared that was the case. I was concerned because nothing about Jonah or his attitudes provided any corollary to my situation.

Then I read about Isaiah's call in Isaiah 6. Voila! That type of call resonated with me. This time we see God extending a call that sounds like it could be answered by anyone, "Who will go, and whom shall I send?" And Isaiah answered him, "Here am I, send me!" Isaiah 6 fits me far better than Jonah's story. Is there any reason for us to assume that God has only one way to call people into service? It (his style) can and does reflect the uniqueness of the person to whom he calls? I assert that he can and does operate in this way.

We have inherited a unique relationship with Abba Father who knows all about us, and custom designed us in every intimate detail. Revelation 2:17 tells us that one day Jesus will give each of us a new name, indicative of the unique relationship we have shared with him. Interaction between the Lord and each one of us is specialized. We can rejoice in the unique connection we have with our God and Father.

Scriptures showing God's unique dealings with individuals

- Solomon's prayer of dedication of the Temple asking God to *"Forgive and act; deal with each man according to all he does, since you know his heart (for you alone know the hearts of all men).* 1 Kings 8:38-39, NIV
- Collected all my tears…recorded each one in your book. Psalm 56:8
- Tell Him each one of your concerns. Psalm 62:8
- You render to each one according to his work. Psalm 62:12
- Blessed is the man who trusts in you. Psalm 84:11-12
- I want them back every last one who bears my name, every man, woman, and child I created for my glory – I made each one. Isaiah 43:5 (The Message)
- I will carefully watch each one of you. Ezekiel 34:7
- Live as you are called – God called each one. 1 Corinthians 7:17

- "He calls his own sheep by name and leads them out." John 10:3

Questions to Consider:

1. When we read David's prayer to God in Psalm 139, he recounts the way God fashioned him in his mother's womb. What does it mean to you to see the intricate way God deals with every detail of our beings and our lives?

2. When you notice all the things that are unique and one of a kind (like snowflakes, fingerprints, etc.) what does that tell you about God's creative power?

3. What's the main problem with "one size fits all" in most things?

4. Have you ever heard a stirring testimony about a person's conversion to Christ? Was that story the same as your own testimony or different from yours?

5. How do you respond to the concept of God's unique dealings with each one of us?

6. When Jesus said the very hairs on our heads are numbered, what was he telling us about the nature of God's care? (Luke 12:37)

7. In Psalm 56:8 we read, "…you have collected all my tears and recorded every one of them in your book…" What does that suggest about the intimacy of God's concern over each of us?

8. When Jesus describes himself as the good shepherd in John 10 he said something that described how intimately he knows each sheep. What did he say? (John 10:3)

Chapter 7: Joint Heirs with Christ

Key Scripture: Romans 8:17, *"Now if we are children, then we are heirs—heirs of God and co-heirs with Christ, if indeed we share in his sufferings in order that we may also share in his glory."*

Because of our connection with God we have inherited an equally profound interconnection with Christ who is God's son. We are told about this interconnection in Romans. *"For you did not receive a spirit that makes you a slave again to fear, but you received the Spirit of sonship. And by him we cry, "Abba, Father." The Spirit himself testifies with our spirit that we are God's children. Now if we are children, then we are heirs – heirs of God and co-heirs with Christ, if indeed we share in his sufferings in order that we may also share in his glory"* (Romans 8:15-17).

You will notice that this verse mentions the Father, Son (Christ), and Holy Spirit. This is one of several New Testament scriptures that refer directly to all three persons in the Godhead. Not only does this reinforce the teaching about the Trinity in the Bible, but it also allows us to see that interaction with each person automatically involves the other two. Though we might pull them apart for the purpose of literary examination, we cannot actually separate them. Interaction with one is interaction with the whole. There is no way, for example, to pray to the Father to the exclusion of the Son and Spirit. You might seemingly accomplish a feat like that in your mind, but not in reality.

So far, we have looked at the ways we are wrapped up in God, and focused on the presence of the indwelling Holy Spirit. Now, we will give attention to the ways we are connected inextricably to Christ himself. The Apostle Paul referred to God's ministry among the Gentiles (that includes us) as "Christ in you, the hope of glory" (Colossians 1:27). From this verse we are introduced to one of our important connections to Christ, namely, the fact that Christ is in us.

Christ in You

Having looked at the indwelling presence of the Holy Spirit, we know that God planted Christ in us in the form of the Holy Spirit. The Holy Spirit dwells within us in direct connection to our own spirits. In fact, the Holy Spirit's presence is synonymous with Christ in us. From Romans 5-8 we learn five important ways we have been realigned, through dying with Christ on the cross, and being raised up to a new life with Him. We have been realigned in these ways:

- **From Adam's race to God's family:** Romans 5 is a treatise on the shift accomplished because of the finished work of Christ on the cross. Paul explained, *"For as in Adam all die, even so in Christ shall all be made alive* (I Corinthians 15:22, NIV). By default, every human is a descendant of Adam's race, which puts all under a curse of separation from God due to sin. Those who participate with Christ in his death, burial, and resurrection, are realigned from Adam's race to God's family through their connection to Christ.

- **From slavery to sin to a servant of Christ:** Romans 6 explains that our default condition was slavery to sin. Baptism is a representation of our own death with Christ. We died enslaved to sin and were resurrected as slaves of Christ. Paul wrote, *"Don't you know that when you offer yourselves to someone to obey them as slaves, you are slaves to the one whom you obey – whether you are slaves to sin, which leads to death, or to obedience, which leads to righteousness?"* (Romans 6:16). Bob Dylan wrote a song about this principle with these words, "Well, It may be the Devil, or it may be the Lord, but everybody's gonna' serve somebody." In our default state there was no choice about whom we would serve. Slavery to sin was the default condition. We were removed from that default condition by dying with Christ. We were resurrected as willing slaves of Christ.

- **From married to the Law to married to Christ:** Romans 7 compares marriage to the Law which can only condemn us to being married to Christ (part of the bride of Christ which is the church), which frees us from the impossible demands of the Law. As before, the transition point is our death along with Christ. Paul wrote that the Law is in force as long as we live, but that we can and do die to the law in our connection to Christ. As the bride of Christ we discover that everything Christ might demand of us, He does within us. He, himself, is the power behind everything he calls us to be.

- **From the mind on the flesh to the mind on the Spirit:** Romans 8 is the victory chapter of Paul's theological treatise on justification by faith. He lets us know that the default condition of a mind continually focused on the flesh, will lead inexorably to death. This is the only option for all who are in Adam. Through our connection to Christ we are enabled to focus our minds on the Holy Spirit, and the result is life and peace.

In all four situations above, the default condition is not optional. Our condition as a descendant of Adam's race is hopeless and helpless. Because of that separated condition we were slaves of sin, married to the law, and stuck with our minds focused on the flesh. When we divested ourselves from that sad state through our co-death with Christ and our resurrection with him we inherited all that we enjoy by being connected to Christ. We are now in God's family, slaves of Christ, married to Christ (as part of the bride of Christ – the church), and having our minds freed to be able to focus on the indwelling Spirit.

You in Christ: (Seated with Christ)

It is meaningful to know that Christ is within you, but we also need to see that we are with and in Christ which places us where he is. So where is Christ? We know that he is seated next to the Father in the throne room of heaven (Ephesians 1:20-22). So if we are in Christ, then where are we? Ephesians 2:6 tells us, *"And God raised us up with Christ and seated us with him in the heavenly realms in Christ Jesus…"* What does that mean? It means that though our physical bodies are here on earth, our spirits enjoy the heavenly perspective of being seated with Christ in the heavenly places. This means that our eternal lives have already begun. Because we are in Christ we are secure in our connection to him by being with him in heaven.

Is this really true of us? Consider Paul's statement in Colossians 3:1-3 *"Since, then, you have been raised with Christ, set your hearts on things above, where Christ is seated at the right hand of God. Set your minds on things above, not earthly things. For you died, and your life is now hidden with Christ in God. When Christ, who is your life, appears, then you also will appear with him in glory."*

This is not a matter of playing mind games. Our real lives are hidden with Christ in God. Because he is in us, what happened to him 2,000 years ago also happened to us. Because we are in him, we are, in essence, seated next to him in heaven. Talk about a heavenly perspective! We don't have to worry about losing salvation when it has already begun for us. We can visualize ourselves as already with Christ in heaven!

Christ as our "Yes and Amen"

Paul makes a fascinating statement about Christ in 2 Corinthians 1:19-20. He wrote, "For the Son of God, Jesus Christ, who was preached among you by me and Silas and Timothy, was not "Yes" and "No," but in him it has always been "Yes." For no matter how many promises God has made, they are "Yes" in Christ. And so through him the "Amen" is spoken by us to the glory of God." An understanding of this passage requires a basic understanding of the Hebrew word "Amen" often translated as "so be it." Not only was that word used as a declaration of affirmation, but it often signified that something was certain, sure, valid, and true.

When Jesus taught during his earthly ministry he would often precede something he was about to say by saying "Amen" (Translated as "Verily" in the King James), and in John's gospel we sometimes see him saying Amen twice in a row ("Verily, Verily I say unto thee"). By making such a statement, Jesus is giving an oath of sorts as to the truthfulness and reliability of what he is about to say. He is giving an "amen" or perhaps even a double amen to his own teaching. Say anything in the Hebrew language twice in a row and you are saying it with emphasis and passion.

Furthermore, we notice the use of "amen" in conjunction with God as proof of his powerful and reliable nature. In Isaiah 65:16 God is called the "God of Amen." Anyone who invokes a blessing or makes an oath in the land under God's authority is doing so in the sight of the God of Amen who is the God of truth. What is ascribed to the Father in the Old Testament is also ascribed to the Son in Revelation 3:14 where we read Jesus' words in his letter to the church in Laodicea, *"These are the words of the Amen, the faithful and true witness, the ruler of God's creation."* From this we notice that both Father and Son are "Amen". This is a powerful, yet largely unknown aspect of the deity of both Father and Son. It means that they are faithful, true, certain, valid, reliable, dependable, trustworthy, etc.

So what happens when someone who is the "Amen" makes a promise to you? Naturally, you can count on it to come to pass. The Bible is full of such promises and Jesus is the "amen" who makes them all as good as accomplished already. Among all the things we have inherited in our treasure chest of precious promises, we have Jesus himself as our "Yes and Amen".

Living in a world that so often tells us "no" to every request we make, it is refreshing to finally encounter someone whose modus operandi is "yes and amen". Years ago, when I first arrived at my new ministry, a youth sponsor asked me about painting a Jr. High class room. Without hesitation, I replied off the cuff, "Sure, why not." The youth sponsor got a surprised look on her face and said, "Wow that was easy. That's the first time I've had anyone say "Yes" to anything I've asked around here. Usually, I'm told it will have to be decided by the board, and I end up giving up on anything ever being done." I found out what it was like to be someone's "yes and amen," and I was glad to be able to do that for her.

Jesus is our "Yes and Amen." All God's promises are mirrored in the face of Jesus who is bold to say "Amen" and perhaps even "Amen, Amen." This is an inheritance that is sure and reliable for us.

It also enables us to shout "amen." to the words of Jesus as we see them coming to fruition in our own lives.

Questions to Consider:

1. What does it mean to be a joint heir with Christ? What do we share together?

2. If Christ is living within you, how can you be more aware of His presence?

3. What is the default condition of the unbeliever? Why is this a problem?

4. What four changes take place when an unbeliever allows Christ to come into his life?

5. What does it mean to be married to the Law (Romans 7:1-6). What situation is preferable to this condition?

6. What does it mean to be seated with Christ in the heavenly places (Ephesians 2:6)?

7. Can you testify to a time when Jesus was able to come through as "yes and amen" in your life?

8. Why is it important to see yourself as "in Christ" and also important to see Christ as "in you"?

Chapter 8: The Authority in the Name of Christ

Key Scriptures: John 14:13-14 (NIV), *"And I will do whatever you ask in my name, so that the Son may bring glory to the Father. You may ask me for anything in my name, and I will do it."*

As our population ages, an increasing number of elderly parents are giving their adult children, power of attorney. Diminished capacities of the parents call for children, or even grand-children, to take on the tasks of paying bills, making medical decisions, handling assets, or drawing up living wills for the parents. In essence, the parent lends his own name to the child, so the son or daughter can act on behalf of the aging parent. Amazingly, Jesus has provided the authority of his name to his followers. The power and authority of Jesus' name is an astounding part of our glorious inheritance.

Authority in the Name of Jesus

John's gospel records Jesus' words to his disciples about the authority that rests in his name. Jesus gave his disciples the power to use his name in ministry. On the night of his betrayal, Jesus revealed to his men the power of his name and gave them his permission to use that name authoritatively. Jesus told his men, *"And I will do whatever you ask in my name, so that the Son may bring glory to the Father. You may ask me for anything in my name, and I will do it"* (John 14:13-14).

Having made this remarkable statement he went on to say, *"You did not choose me, but I chose you and appointed you to go and bear fruit...fruit that will last. Then the Father will give you whatever you ask in my name"* (John 15:16).

In saying this, Jesus reiterated what he said earlier about his name. At the same time, he connected the power of his name with his earlier description of himself as the vine and his followers as the branches. Once again we see that connection provides authority. But Jesus was not finished. Again he told his men, *"In that day you will no longer ask me anything. I tell you the truth, my Father will give you whatever you ask in my name. Until now you have not asked for anything in my name. Ask and you will receive, and your joy will be complete"* (John 16:23-24).

Jesus went on to compare his future suffering to the circumstance of a woman giving birth. In spite of the birth pains, the woman experiences joy once the child is born. Jesus told his men that once his death, burial, and resurrection were accomplished their joy would be complete. Intertwined with all of this discourse was the recurring theme of power in the name of Jesus.

Some see the granting of authority to use the name of Jesus as applying only to the 12 apostles in the upper room. While I am aware of that limiting application of the power to use Jesus' name, I would ask the reader to consider both the context of this promise of power in the name of Jesus and the scriptural examples of using Jesus' name.

In John 13-17, which is John's complete account of the last supper, Jesus gave his men many promises that are not generally seen as applying only to those 12 men:

- Jesus promised to return from heaven to get his people (John 14:2-3).
- Jesus promised to send the Holy Spirit to take his place (John 14:16-18, 26).
- He also promised that He and the Father would come in to dwell in whoever loves him (John 14:23).
- Jesus spoke about his peace which he is leaving with his followers (John 14:27).
- He said he is the true vine and we are the branches (John 15:1-8).
- Jesus spoke about his joy that might remain in his followers (John 15:11).
- He spoke about laying down his life for his friends (John 15:13).

- Jesus commanded that his followers would love one another (John 15:17)
- He spoke about persecution of those who follow him (John 15:19-21).
- As Jesus prayed for unity in John 17, He prayed explicitly, first for the men in the upper room, and then for all who would believe in him through their word (John 17:20-24).

Much of what Jesus said at the last supper has a broader application than to the 12 in the upper room. This indicates a strong likelihood that Jesus' promise of power in his name is a gift to the church at large.

The second consideration requires discovery of New Testament examples in which others, besides the 12 Apostles, minister in the name and authority of Jesus' name. We will also explore scriptural admonitions for believers to minister or pray in Jesus' name. These examples are listed as follows:

- Non Apostles ministering in Jesus' name:
    - An un-named man was casting out demons in Jesus name. Jesus' men urged Jesus to stop the man. *"'Do not stop him,' Jesus said. No one who does a miracle in my name can in the next moment say anything bad about me, for whoever is not against us is for us"* (Mark 9:39).
    - Philip the evangelist worked miracles and preached in the name of Jesus (Acts 8:12-13).
- New Testament admonitions for believers with regards to the name, authority, or power of Jesus Christ available for the use of believers:
    - *Now to him who is able to do immeasurably more than all we ask or imagine, according to his power that is at work within us ...* (Ephesians 3:20)

- *And whatever you do, whether in word or deed, do it all in the name of the Lord Jesus, giving thanks to God the Father through him* (Colossians 3:17).

- *Dear friends, if our hearts do not condemn us, we have confidence before God and receive from him anything we ask, because we obey his commands and do what pleases him. And this is his command: to believe in the name of his Son, Jesus Christ, and to love one another as he commanded us* (1 John 3:21-23).

- *"Again, I tell you that if two of you on earth agree about anything you ask for, it will be done for you by my Father in heaven. For where two or three come together in my name, there am I with them"* (Matthew 18:19-20).

- *Jesus replied, "I tell you the truth, if you have faith and do not doubt, not only can you do what was done to the fig tree, but also you can say to this mountain, 'Go, throw yourself into the sea,' and it will be done. If you believe, you will receive whatever you ask for in prayer"* (Matthew 21:22).

Philippians 2 gives an admonition to us to have the same attitude as Christ Jesus who humbled himself while on earth and endured the cross. Then Philippians 2:9-10 states, *"Therefore God exalted him to the highest place and gave him the name that is above every name, that at the name of Jesus every knee should bow, in heaven and on earth and under the earth ..."* On the basis of this passage, I conclude that when Jesus ascended into heaven, he was given a name of surpassing power.

Before Jesus death, Jesus' disciples called him various names of respect. They called him "teacher" (Rabbi), "master", even "Lord." These titles were in common use. Acts 9:5 records unconverted Saul of Tarsus calling Jesus "Lord" without knowing who he was addressing. When Saul asked, "Who are you Lord?" he was simply using a term of respect. After his conversion, the Apostle Paul called Jesus "Lord" in an entirely new way. In fact, he repeatedly called himself a servant of the Lord Jesus (Romans 1:1, Galatians 1:10). Paul understood that Jesus possesses a name that is above every other name.

Sadly, there are many who are oblivious to the holy power and authority of Jesus' name. In the same way that many take God's name in vain, there are many who demean the name of Jesus, using it as an expletive in casual conversation. I am confident that they will change their tune when they bow the knee before Christ and confess him as Lord to the glory of God (Philippians 2:10-11).

What, then, is the truth about the power of Jesus' name? Does the name of Christ carry power like a magic incantation or rubbing a magic lamp? Do Christians gain the ability to invoke Jesus' name in order to work their own magic? Some assume as much, and in doing so they confer upon themselves the ability to dominate God, making Him subservient to an incantation. The name of Jesus is powerful, but it is not a plaything for us to use in order to achieve our own ends.

Acts 19 gives the example of certain Jews who tried to invoke the name of the Lord Jesus to drive out demons. The seven sons of a high priest named Sceva said to a demon possessed man, *"In the name of Jesus whom Paul preaches, I command you to come out"* (Acts 19:13). In response, the demon acknowledged that he knew Jesus and Paul, but demanded, *"Who are you?"* and then jumped on the men and overpowered them all, giving them such a beating they ran out of the house naked and bleeding (Acts 19:16). That day these brothers learned that the name of Jesus was not a magic incantation for anyone to use as they please. They had seen the apostles use that name with power, but the same authority did not belong to them.

Likewise we are not free to turn the name of Jesus into our own plaything to use any way we like. We must not mistake the authority of Jesus' name as being under our dominion as believers. On the contrary, we are fully under His dominion as servants. Jesus is the head of the church and each of us make up parts of the body (Romans 12:5, 1 Corinthians 12:12-27, Ephesians 4:11-16).

So what does that name of Jesus represent? It represents Jesus' own power and authority. We know from scripture that Christ was not only raised from the dead, but also seated by God at his right hand in the heavenly realms (Eph. 1:20-23). In that exalted position, Jesus serves as high priest, and mediator between man and God (1

Timothy 2:5, Hebrews 7:24-28; 8:6). In this exalted position, the name of Jesus has even greater power and authority than he had during his earthly ministry. That name, and His corresponding presence, is available for the ministries of the church.

How can the church minister under that name of Jesus?

- **In Prayer and supplication** (John 14:13-14, John 15:16, John 16:23-24, 26): We have already looked at what Jesus told his men at the Last Supper. The promise Jesus gave was meant for them as apostles, and for use in the church which would follow soon after. Because we are in the church, we may also pray using the name of Jesus. We pray under His authority, even as we are seated next to Jesus Christ in the heavenly places (Ephesians 2:6). We often pray "in Jesus' name" as a matter of religious habit, not realizing that we have been entrusted with the surpassing power of His name to accomplish His will. Intercession in the name of Jesus is meant to be a primary ministry of the church, to bring the power of Jesus into action.

- **In Spiritual warfare** (Mark 16:17, Luke 9:49-50, Luke 10:17, Ephesians 6:18): The gospels give many examples of Jesus casting out demons. His disciples also rejoiced in being able to cast out demons in Jesus' name (Luke 10:17). We tend to look at these events and assume that such ministry was only for the time when Jesus lived on earth. However, Ephesians 6 instructs us in spiritual warfare, and calls us to stand firm in the victory which Christ has given us (Ephesians 6:10-13). Furthermore, we can pray offensively as well as defensively in the name of Jesus. Perhaps we would use Jesus' name more if we understood how Jesus intended for us to use that name. James reminds us that we have not because we ask not (James 4:3). If we understand the power available for us in Jesus name we will employ that power in prayer, in spiritual battle, in intercession and in ministry.

- **In the church** (Matthew 18:18-20): This intriguing passage focuses on the church's ministry of binding and loosing on earth what God wishes to bind and loose in heaven. In fact, the account in Matthew 18:15-17 give a specific example of the general principle of binding and loosing. We are often remedial in our understanding and practice of this important ministry, because we fail to see this passage as instructive for us in our day. There is tremendous power when two or three agree together on anything in prayer. Such directed prayer can loosen many things that have been bound up, and bind up whatever is in opposition to the ministry of the church. Perhaps we endure many struggles and blockages in the church because we don't know how to pray offensively under the authority of His name.

- **In ministry and benevolence** (Matthew 18:5, Mark 9:37, Mark 9:39, Mark 9:41): Peter and John give a fascinating example of ministry in the name of Christ in Acts 3 where they healed the crippled beggar. Notice Peter's words to the beggar, *"Silver or gold I do not have, but what I have I give you. In the name of Jesus Christ of Nazareth, walk."* We tend to confine healings such as this one to its day and time because such miracles gave credence to the veracity of the Apostles' teaching. We assume such things cannot happen these days. I contend that we are largely ignorant of what can be done in the name of Jesus. In James 5:14-15 those who are sick are instructed to call for the elders who can anoint them with oil and pray the prayer of faith for healing. The elders of our church have participated in this ministry often, believing in the power of Jesus to heal.

I believe that the authoritative name of Jesus our Lord is available for the ministry of the church. Perhaps the effectual power of Jesus' name is a part of our inheritance that has been diminished due to lack of use in the modern church. Years ago I read a book by Watchman Nee called <u>The Prayer Ministry of the Church.</u> It opened my eyes not only to the prayer ministry of the church, but also to the power available under the authority of Jesus' name.

In many churches these days, the ministry of prayer has been relegated to the back burners of church life. What makes this so distressing is that no other organization, group, club, or ministry has been given that task that was assigned to the church. If the church does not pray who else will do it? We are entrusted with the ministry of prayer, and empowered to pray in Christ's name. Furthermore, we are promised that the gates of hell itself cannot prevail against the church when we do what we have been called to do by God. This is a day when the church needs to recover the ministry of prayer in Jesus' name.

In 1970 when visiting a town named Ballarat, Australia for a revival meeting, an Australian Minister named John Timms told me that the dynamic for ministry in his church came largely from four elderly women who prayed every day for him and his ministry in the Peel St. Church of Christ. As a 20 year old I was more inclined to rely on the natural capabilities of skillful and talented Christian workers. I didn't see anything major to be gained in a prayer closet when a motivated worker could surely make it all happen with grit, determination, and action. Now, 40 years later, I fully understand the wisdom in his words. I wish that prayer had been a greater focus for my early ministry. I no longer underestimate the power in the prayers of the congregation. These days, I see the work of prayer warriors in our congregation in an entirely new light. May their tribe increase!

Questions to Consider:

1. At the Last Supper, what did Jesus tell his men they could do in his name? (John 14:13-14, John 15:16, John 16:23-24)

2. When did Jesus Christ receive a name that is higher than any other name? (Philippians 2:9-10)

3. What did Jesus' disciples call him during his earthly ministry?

4. In what ways can the church labor under the name of Jesus Christ?

5. What do you consider to be the most important aspect of the authority of the Name of Jesus?

6. What is the danger of misusing the name of Jesus Christ? (Acts 19:13-16)

7. How do we conduct spiritual warfare under the authority of Jesus Christ? (Ephesians 6:10-13,18)

8. When Matthew 18:18-20 covered the matter of binding and loosing on earth and in heaven what was it talking about?

Chapter 9: The Glory of Christ: Past Present and Future

Key Verses: Psalm 2:8-9, *"Ask of me, and I will make the nations your inheritance, the ends of the earth your possession. You will rule them with an iron scepter; you will dash them to pieces like pottery."*

The Old Testament scriptures gave a picture of the Messiah that was confusing to those who studied it. For example, there were passages in Isaiah that pointed to a coming king who will reign in might and justice (Isaiah 9:6-7, 11:1-10, 33:17-22, 42:1-4,). Other passages, however, speak of a suffering servant who is rejected, beaten, and killed (Isaiah 50:4-7, 51:21-23, 52:14, 53:2-12). Many who studied these Messianic passages could not imagine such opposite situations referring to the same person. Some even concluded that the passages concerning the suffering servant were about the suffering of the Jewish people throughout history.

Looking back on Isaiah, we know that the same Messiah was the subject of both texts. Jesus was the suffering servant in his first coming to earth to put on flesh and live his life as a humble carpenter's son from Nazareth. His life was seemingly cut short by arrest, beatings, and crucifixion. The reigning king passages will typify his return to earth in future glory. Everything Isaiah prophesied about the Messiah either came true in his first appearing, or will come true at his second appearing. What the Jews of Jesus' day didn't understand was that the Messiah would come to earth two times.

His Earthly Glory

Jesus' first appearance to live as a man for 33 years on earth was glorious. But it wasn't glorious in the way the people were expecting it to be. The Jews, living under Roman oppression, were anxious for a political savior to come and defeat the tyranny of Roman rule. They were hoping for a successful rebellion to restore the kingdom of Israel to what it had been under King David and Solomon. Jesus had no intention to be that kind of savior. The kingdom he preached was a heavenly kingdom that would change people from the inside out. Jesus came to earth as a humble servant to do whatever his Father in heaven desired of him. Even his death on the cross was glorious, but not the kind of glory that would impress the crowds of that day.

The glory of the incarnate Savior was a glory wrapped up and concealed in flesh. Certainly, it was glorious to observe his powerful and authoritative preaching. His miracles and healings were glorious. But his true glory was covered over by his earthly body. Jesus gave Peter, James and John the opportunity to observe his true glory for a brief moment on top of a lonely mountain (Matthew 17, Mark 9, Luke 9) where he was "transfigured" before them. The text says that *"his face shone like the sun and his clothes became as white as the light"* (Matthew 17:2). It seems that the fleshly covering that hid his true glory was removed temporarily so that what was true of Jesus could be seen by human eyes.

This amazing revelation was not shared by the twelve disciples, but only available to the inner circle, who were told not to speak about what they had witnessed until after Jesus' resurrection (Matthew 17: 9). What these men had seen had a profound impact on them and their ministries. But the glory of the incarnate Christ was not the apex of Jesus' glory. There were greater things yet to come.

His Heavenly Glory

What was true of the glory of the Incarnate Jesus is now even greater in scope for the Heavenly Jesus. While on earth Jesus was the obedient servant of his heavenly Father who did nothing on his own, but only what he saw his Father doing (John 8:28, 42). After Jesus' death, burial, resurrection, and ascension several things changed for him:

- He exchanged the hidden glory covered by his earthly body for the glory he had in heaven before he put on earthly flesh (Hebrews 1:3).

- He was exalted to the highest place where he is now seated beside the Heavenly Father (Philippians 2:9; Ephesians 1:20-21; Hebrews 1:3).

- He received a name that is above every other name (Philippians 2:9-11; Ephesians 1:21; Hebrews 1:4).

- He became head over all things, especially over the church which is his body (Ephesians 1:20-23; Philippians 2:10-11; Colossians 1:17-19).

- He operates in heaven as the eternal Great High Priest and intermediary between God and man (Hebrews 4:14-5:10; 1 Timothy 2:5; Hebrews 9:15).

The glory of the incarnate Christ is true in even greater magnitude in the heavenly Christ who is seated beside the Father in the heavenly places. This is a glorious inheritance for Jesus who has completed the work of redemption and is able to take his seat beside the father. And, as joint heirs with Christ we also enjoy an inheritance coming from Christ's finished work. Hebrews 9:15 reminds us, *"For this reason Christ is the mediator of a new covenant, that those who are called may receive the promised eternal inheritance—now that he has died as a ransom to set them free from the sins committed under the first covenant."*

The Impact of Christ's glory on us

The glory of Christ operates as a change agent within us. Having mentioned this before, I am excited to repeat the principle of transformation given in 2 Corinthians 3:18 where we are told, *"And we, who with unveiled faces all reflect the Lord's glory, are being transformed into his likeness with ever-increasing glory, which comes from the Lord, who is the Spirit."* Our ability to see the glory of Christ without any veils hiding that glory from us has a transforming power over us making us more like Him little by little every day. For this reason, the glory of Christ is meaningful to us, and worthy of our full attention. We can focus on the personality of our Savior daily, and have confidence that he is transforming us to become like him.

It is amazing to consider that the Shekinah Glory of God that rested above the mercy seat on the Ark of the Covenant in the Holy of Holies of the Tabernacle and Temple. It is a glory that was present within Jesus during his time on earth. That same glory also carried by the Holy Spirit (Christ in you, the hope of Glory) has been planted within us. Our bodies have become temples of God (1 Corinthians. 6:19-20) which makes us carriers of the glory of Christ planted within us. This glory is not ours to control, but it is a glory we are privileged to observe whenever we mortify our flesh so that the resurrected Jesus can rise up within us and do what only he can do through us. It is the glory of Christ living within us that transforms us so that we can reflect the glory of Christ within us.

This glory can also be sensed by others around us. Paul wrote in 2 Corinthians 2:14-16 that we are the aroma of Christ. Imagine that! We smell like Jesus! And that aroma can be inhaled by both the saved and lost around us. We have something within us that is a glorious treasure (2 Corinthians 4:7). It is also something we can share with others if we are willing to let it be seen within us. The glory of the indwelling Christ is a powerful part of our inheritance. It not only changes us, but impacts others around us if we allow it to be reflected in us.

His Future Glory

Having looked at Jesus Incarnate Glory and his current Heavenly Glory there is still another aspect of Christ's glory to view. The New Testament has much to say about the return of Christ to rule over the kingdoms of the earth. There is debate among various Christian traditions as to the timing of Christ's return, the elements of the time line regarding that event, and the way that Christ's return will impact the world stage. Not wanting to alienate some readers by presenting one side over another in the eschatological (end times) debate, I prefer to focus on Christ's glory as the returning King. One thing can be said regarding Christ's return without stirring up divisive disputes. He is returning to rule. That much is settled in most

Christian circles. We learn certain things about Christ's return from the scriptures:

- **The Rider on the White Horse** (Revelation 19:11-21) Part of the glory that is revealed about Christ in this passage includes:
  - the **various titles** Jesus wears here including:
    - ✓ Faithful and True (vs. 11)
    - ✓ A name written on him that no one but he himself knows (vs. 12)
    - ✓ The Word of God (vs. 13)
    - ✓ King of Kings and Lord of Lords (vs. 16)
  - The **visual aspects** of the rider on the white horse (vs. 11-21)
    - ✓ Originating from heaven (vs. 11)
    - ✓ Coming forth to judge and make war (vs. 11)
    - ✓ Eyes like blazing fire (vs. 12)
    - ✓ Wearing many crowns (vs. 12)
    - ✓ Wearing a robe dipped in blood (vs. 13)
    - ✓ The armies of heaven follow him (vs. 14)
    - ✓ A sharp sword comes from his mouth (vs. 15)
      - Killing all the enemy armies (vs. 21)
      - The beast and false prophet thrown alive into fiery lake (vs. 20)
- **Christ as the Judge** (Revelation 20:11-15)
  - Judging all the dead, great and small (vs. 12)

- Books were opened and the Book of Life (vs. 12)
- Death, hades, and all not written in the Book of Life thrown in the lake of fire (vs. 14-15)

- **God Almighty and The Lamb in the New Jerusalem** (Revelation 21 & 22)
    - Titles of Jesus
        - ✓ Alpha and Omega, The Beginning and the End (vs. 6)
        - ✓ The Lamb (vs. 9, 22)
        - ✓ The Root and Offspring of David, and the bright Morning Star (22:16)
        - ✓ The Spirit and the bride (vs. 17)
        - ✓ Maranatha (Come Lord Jesus) (vs. 20)

Though much more could be said concerning the return of Christ, this is sufficient to show the glory that will be revealed when Jesus returns to conquer all who oppose God, to judge everyone as the righteous judge, and to rule beside God Almighty in the New Jerusalem. All who inherit eternal life in heaven will see the full glory of both the Father and the Son together as the light and temple in the heavenly city. (Revelation 21:22-25)

Considering the glory that is to come I am reminded of the benediction found in 1 Peter 5:10-11, "*And the God of all grace, who called you to his eternal glory in Christ, after you have suffered a little while, will himself restore you and make you strong, firm and steadfast. To him be the power for ever and ever. Amen.*"

It is this eternal glory that is part of our glorious inheritance. We can rejoice to get a glimpse of all that will be available to us when Christ comes back in his full glory. Let us echo the closing words of the book of Revelation. Maranatha! Come Lord Jesus!

Questions to Consider:

1. When Isaiah prophesied the coming of a ruling king, and also told of an obedient servant who would be beaten and killed, why was it difficult to consider both prophecies as referring to the coming Messiah?

2. What was the nature of Jesus' glory while he lived on earth?

3. What is the most glorious aspect of Christ in heaven today?

4. Why is the glory of Christ important to us today (2 Corinthians 3:18)?

5. Apostle Paul writes that we are like clay pots with treasure inside us. What is the nature of that treasure? (2 Corinthians 4:7)

6. Considering the future glory of Christ, what aspect of his return seems the most glorious to you?

7. Can you think of any ways in which seeing the glory of Christ with an unveiled face has brought about changes within you to make you more like Christ? (2 Corinthians 3:18)

8. What would you like to be able to say to Christ Jesus when you see Him face to face for the first time? What do you long to hear him say to you?

Chapter 10: Appropriating our Inheritance by Faith

Key Scripture: Matthew 7:7, *"Ask and it will be given to you; seek and you will find; knock and the door will be opened to you. For everyone who asks receives; he who seeks finds; and to him who knocks, the door will be opened."*

Our inheritance from God is based on his promises, but we have a task before us of appropriating those promises by faith. We know that by faith we not only believe that God exists but we also believe that he is the rewarder of those who diligently seek Him (Hebrews 11:6). Jesus taught that those who ask shall be given; those who seek shall find, and those who knock will have the door opened unto them (Matthew 7:7). In each example there is an action on our part and a corresponding action by God. If we diligently seek God, He rewards us. If we ask, God gives. If we seek, God sees to it that we find. If we knock, God opens the door. The appropriation of God's power through our faith involves our part and God's part. Both are necessary.

The Apostle Paul instructs us to *"be strong in the Lord and in His mighty power"* (Ephesians 6:10). Here we notice a command to stand in the power of Christ. The Lord is not grudging in his promises. We don't need to squeeze power out of a reluctant deity who is too stingy to share His resources with his children. God is more than willing to give His strength to His redeemed. Your job as a child of God is not to endlessly plead for power, but to begin acting in His power. Faith goes beyond asking to acting. By faith you act on the fact that "His mighty power" is yours through Christ.

It is also true that if you are in Christ, all the victorious dynamic of his resurrection belongs to you. Christ's triumph over Satan becomes your triumph as well. You can appropriate that victory by faith and make it real in your own life.

The Meaning of Appropriation

Appropriation involves setting aside something to a special purpose, or taking possession of something we have a right to own. Through faith we are able to appropriate God's power and promises, thereby experiencing God's provision as our own possession. We are not talking about occult magic arts. This is not "abra cadabra" talk. It is a matter of appropriating the realities of our spiritual inheritance.

The dictionary gives various definitions for "appropriate". In this context, appropriation is taking something for one's exclusive use, or setting something aside for a specific use by a person, group, or organization. The term "appropriation" is often used in the context of the work of government. Perhaps you may have heard of the "House and Senate Appropriations Committee." These committees of the Congress are the ones who make decisions to set aside money for specific purposes. When Congress makes the proper appropriations through these committees, the money is set aside for the exclusive use of the departments to which funds were appropriated.

If, for example, the Congress were to set aside 700 billion dollars for the Defense Department, then the Pentagon knows it has permission to spend that amount of money for defense purposes in the year in which it is appropriated. Every department knows that if they don't actually spend all the money that has been appropriated to them, they run the very real risk of losing that appropriation the next year. This is why it's common practice in most governmental departments to go on a spending spree at the end of the fiscal year, in an attempt to use every last appropriated dollar.

There are always two actions in any appropriation. The provider does something to set aside funds for the use of the receiver. Then the receiver must take action to make use of that which has been appropriated. If the provider fails to appropriate, then, there is nothing available to use. If the receiver fails to appropriate, then the appropriation does them no good whatsoever. Failure to act on either part nullifies the appropriation.

In spiritual terms, the believer must first seek to learn what God has appropriated to him. Then, by faith, he must make use of that which has been appropriated. We can appropriate by faith anything God has appropriated by His promises. Our faith in any promise of God is demonstrated when we appropriate that promise. In 2 Peter 1:4 we read, *"Through these he has given us his very great and precious promises, so that through them you may participate in the divine nature and escape the corruption in the world caused by evil desires."*

We cannot appropriate what God has not promised, but God's promises are more than sufficient for every need. (Barbour Pub. has produced The Bible Promise Book, in both KJV and NIV format with 1,000 Bible promises arranged alphabetically in topics.) Our task is to make use of God's appropriation. Faith is our daily appropriation of God's eternal appropriation.

God's promises are available for every believer in Christ. But they will not automatically benefit every Christian. The promises must be called into experiential reality by daily faith. Faith is what transforms promises into performance. The person who believes puts himself into the promise, personalizes it, and says, "This is true for me right now!" Faith in the promise, and trust in the maker of the promise, is what brings life into the promise, and brings the promise to life. By faith we show that we truly believe that God keeps his word. Without faith we are calling God a liar. When we doubt God's word we are saying, "God may have said it, but he will not do it for me."

Speaking our faith

Jesus said something remarkable in Matthew 21:21-22; 17:20, (NIV) "If you have faith, and do not doubt, you can say to a mountain, 'Remove yourself!' and it will move, Nothing shall be impossible for you." Notice here, that the invitation is to say, not pray. There will be times when what you say is as important as what you pray. Sometimes we need to go beyond just praying about our mountains and begin boldly speaking to them, with the authority of faith, based on God's precious promises, and commanding them to be moved. The promise of Christ is unequivocal. He stated bluntly: tell the mountain to shift out of the way, and it will shift, as long as you speak in faith. Barriers can be removed through the appropriated authority of exercised faith.

We see an example of this by looking at Moses standing at the banks of the Red Sea. The Egyptians are behind him, and his own people are terrified by the only two visible options, death by drowning or slaughter by Egyptians. Moses stood praying to God, and God responded with a rather surprising reprimand. In Exodus 14:15-16 we read, "Then the Lord said to Moses, 'Why are you crying out to me? Tell the Israelites to move on. Raise your staff and stretch out your hand over the sea to divide the water so that the Israelites can go through the sea on dry ground…'" The very thing Moses was praying to receive was what God had already appropriated to him. In that moment, Moses needed to stop praying and start appropriating. God told him to raise his staff and tell the people to move on. What God had already given, Moses simply needed to receive by faith and get on with the business at hand.

Undergoing or Overcoming

Some people appear to be consistent "under-goers". They are constantly undergoing various problems, temptations, bad habits, psychosomatic symptoms, bad attitudes, failures, defeats, etc. When you ask how they are doing they sigh and say, "I'm doing the best I can under the circumstances." This is the crux of the problem. As believers, we have no need to live "under the circumstances". A believer with a defeatist attitude has, in essence, called God a liar. Because of this lack of faith, the spiritual inheritance God has appropriated for them does them absolutely no good in daily experience.

Others live the lives of "overcomers" (see chapter 5). By faith, they appropriate the promised power to live above their circumstances. They apply faith in God's promises to their circumstances and that makes all the difference. By faith they speak to their mountains, and the mountains move. They believe and they receive what has already been set aside for their use. They experience the abundant supply of heaven's resources in the realm of daily life. God calls you to appropriate today, by faith, what He has appropriated for your use. By faith, you can claim this glorious inheritance.

Questions to Consider:

1. What is our part in appropriation and what is God's part?

2. What is the spiritual means of appropriation (1 John 5:4)?

3. What do promises from God have to do with appropriation?

4. When Moses stood before the Red Sea praying to God, what did God tell him to do (Exodus 14:15-16)?

5. Do you generally feel more like an under-goer or an overcomer?

6. We know that prayer is important, but what else is also important along with prayer in the matter of appropriation by faith?

7. What happens if we fail to appropriate by faith on the basis of what God has promised?

Chapter 11: Life in the Kingdom

Key Scripture: Romans 14:17, *"For the kingdom of God is not a matter of eating and drinking, but of righteousness, peace and joy in the Holy Spirit."*

The summation of all things related to our inheritance is revealed in what Jesus preached about the Kingdom of Heaven. Jesus said this of the end times, *"Then the King will say to those on his right, 'Come, you who are blessed by my Father; take your inheritance, the kingdom prepared for you since the creation of the world"* (Matthew 25:34). We might be inclined to assume that this invitation is for a future time in a future location. But the Kingdom of Heaven is here and now.

According to scripture, we are already living in the kingdom of God. We are currently joint heirs with Christ. We are in him and he is in us. All that he has received he has shared with us, even in the here and now. Let me add that the kingdoms has a direct corollary to the church, for Jesus is the king of the kingdom and as well as the head of the church. The people in the kingdom today are also a part of the church which is the bride of Christ.

The initial teachings of Jesus and his disciples dealt with the "nearness" of the kingdom (Matthew 3:2, 4:17, 10:7). People were told to prepare themselves inwardly for the coming of that kingdom. He went on to say that the kingdom is within you (Luke 17:21). A series of parables recorded by Matthew describe the kingdom in a variety of ways.

- Like a man who sowed good seed in his field, Matthew 13:24
- Like a mustard seed which a man took and planted in his field, Matthew 13:31,
- Like yeast which a woman mixed into a large amount of flour, Matthew 13:33,
- Like treasure hidden in a field, Matthew13:44,
- Like a merchant looking for fine pearls, Matthew 13:45,

- Like a net let down into a lake catching all kinds of fish, Matthew 13:47,

- Like an owner of a house bringing out new and old treasures from his storehouse, Matthew 13:52,

- Like a king who wanted to settle accounts with his servants, Matthew 18:23,

- Like a landowner who went out early to hire men to work in his vineyard, Matthew 20:1,

- Like a king who prepared a wedding banquet for his son, Matthew 22:2.

What do these metaphors reveal about the kingdom of God? They introduce a King who is predisposed to fill his kingdom with any and all who want to enter. They describe a Kingdom of inestimable value to all who seek it. They reveal a kingdom that starts out small but grows exponentially. And we learn that this kingdom will permeate what is not of the kingdom and transform it. These parables provide fascinating snapshots of the kingdom Jesus promised during his earthly ministry.

When Pilate questioned Jesus at his trial, Jesus said his kingdom was not of this earth (John 18:36). From this we begin to understand that the kingdom of God is also the kingdom of heaven. That is the kingdom's origin and its source. To simplify, we can state that the kingdom is any place where God reigns as king. Salvation involves leaving the kingdom of darkness and entering into the kingdom of light. Colossians 1:12-14 says, *"...giving thanks to the Father, who has qualified you to share in the inheritance of the saints in the kingdom of light. For he has rescued us from the dominion of darkness and brought us into the kingdom of the Son he loves, in whom we have redemption, the forgiveness of sins."*

With that in mind, The Apostle Paul wrote about the qualities present in that glorious kingdom. In Romans 14:17-18 he wrote, "For the kingdom of God is not a matter of eating and drinking, but of righteousness, peace and joy in the Holy Spirit, because anyone who serves Christ in this way is pleasing to God and approved by men."

Thinking back to what Jesus taught about the kingdom of God, we see Paul continuing that same theme. Paul was in the process of teaching about disputes between stronger and weaker brothers in the faith regarding the eating of meat offered up to idols. Verse 17 is given as a general axiom about the nature of the kingdom of God. It is not about disputes over what to eat or drink, but is all about righteousness, peace, and joy in the Holy Spirit. Let us focus on the qualities which make this kingdom of light so glorious and desirable for those living within it.

Righteousness

Any time the subject of righteousness comes up, the starting place is with God. The Apostle John gives us a glimpse into the throne-room of Heaven in Revelation chapter 4. We cannot help but notice the holiness and purity of the one seated on the throne, with four living creatures surrounding the throne saying day and night, "Holy, Holy, Holy is the Lord God, the Almighty, who was and who is and who is to come" (Revelation 4:8). The kingdom of God is a kingdom of righteousness because God himself is righteous. The gospel carries the subject of righteousness to a great and logical conclusion. Consider this progression:

- God himself is righteous (Romans 1:17),

- God demands righteousness of those who stand before Him (Psalm 1:5-6),

- God provided righteousness in the finished work of Christ on the cross (1 Peter 3:18),

- God preaches righteousness in the gospel (2 Corinthians 5:20),

- God bestows righteousness on those who trust in Christ for salvation (Romans 3:22, 5:17).

Not only is righteousness a central quality in the Kingdom of God, it is also conspicuous in its absence from any other kingdom. Righteousness is not available anywhere outside of God's kingdom.

James Smith wrote about the righteousness found in God's kingdom when he wrote, *"This fig cannot grow on a thistle. It is what the world cannot give"* (Smith, Handfuls on Purpose, Vol.2 p.244). Those who observe the kingdom of God can't help but notice the profound difference between what is godly and what is worldly. That quality might cause an outsider to call people of the kingdom derogatory names such as prudes, do-gooders, goody-two-shoes, etc. The derogatory terms themselves give evidence of the peculiar appearance righteousness has when viewed from outside God's kingdom.

This unique and glorious righteousness from God is imputed to us by grace. The righteousness of God can be seen in our lives as we are changed into the image of Christ, from one degree of glory to the next (2 Corinthians 3:18). Because of Christ, our inheritance of righteousness becomes real in our lives, both now and for eternity.

Peace

Peace is related to righteousness in that one naturally follows after the other. The Greek word, "eirene" has its natural Hebrew counterpart, "shalom". Both refer to absence of strife and peace of mind. Both describe the perfect well-being that comes from being reconciled to God. Because we dwell in a kingdom of righteousness, and because we have been declared righteous ourselves, we are able to be at peace with God and with our fellow believers. Peace encompasses both a God-ward and a man-ward dimension.

The source of righteousness and peace is heavenly. Its outreach creates great blessing within the church. The Hebrew blessing of "shalom" is a continual presence within the family of faith. We are instructed to appropriate this blessing by maintaining peace within the church. Paul gave two memorable admonitions about keeping peace with our brethren. He wrote, *"Make every effort to keep the unity of the Spirit through the bond of peace"* (Ephesians 4:3). In Romans 12:18 he wrote, *"If it is possible, as far as it depends on you, live at peace with everyone."* The peace of God transcends the Kingdom of God and becomes part of our outward ministry in the world. Peace reveals the reality of God's kingdom in the world.

Joy in the Holy Spirit

We notice a sequential relationship between righteousness, peace, and joy. Righteousness and peace are such delightful characteristics that they cannot help but result in joy. Notice, though, that this is joy of a specific kind, joy in the Holy Spirit. This joy is not given by the world and cannot be taken by the world. A search for temporal happiness will never produce the kind of joy that only the Holy Spirit can bring. This kind of joy is not related to circumstance. It is a fruit of the Holy Spirit's presence.

The fruit of the Spirit is specified in Galatians 5:22-23, *"But the fruit of the Spirit is love, joy, peace, patience, kindness, goodness, faithfulness, gentleness and self-control. Against such things there is no law."* The elements of the kingdom mentioned in Romans 14:7 are included as fruit of the Spirit. Both joy and peace make the list, and it isn't much of a stretch to see the corollary between goodness and righteousness.

Righteousness, peace, and joy are not qualities we create within ourselves by human effort. These are among the fruit of life in the Holy Spirit. We may give diligence to preserve these qualities, but we can't produce them from mere fleshly effort.

Furthermore, these qualities are unselfish in nature. They are not individualistic, but rather interdependent, and especially so since the kingdom of God is the domain of the church. The genius of individual kingdom life is the beautiful way it folds into the life of the church. Jesus didn't die on the cross solely for the sake of individual sinners. He gave himself as a sacrifice for the church, to bring her to himself as a bride without spot or wrinkle (Ephesians 5:25-27). Therefore, the kingdom qualities we have just addressed are the same qualities God intends for the world to find dwelling in the life of the church.

Kingdom living characterized by righteousness, peace, and joy in the Holy Spirit is most profoundly demonstrated by the collective faithfulness of the church. This glorious inheritance is available in individual lives, and in the church, not just in the heavenly hereafter, but in the here and now.

Questions to Consider:

1. What part of our inheritance do you think we will receive in heaven, and what part is available for us here and now?

2. Looking at all the ways Jesus described the kingdom in Matthew 13, what was Jesus saying about the Kingdom of God? What is it like to live in that kingdom?

3. Why is the kingdom of God described as a kingdom of righteousness? What will that look like if you are living in that kingdom daily?

4. What kind of peace will we find in the kingdom of God?

5. In what way is joy in the Holy Spirit different than any other kind of joy?

6. How would you describe what it would be like to live daily in a kingdom of righteousness, peace, and joy in the Holy Spirit?

7. Why did Jesus preach so much about the kingdom in the gospels, and what should we learn from Jesus' repeated mention of the kingdom of God in his preaching?

Chapter 12: Defend your Inheritance!

Key Verse Hebrews 12:16, *"See that no one is sexually immoral, or is godless like Esau, who for a single meal sold his inheritance rights as the oldest son."*

When Hebrews gives some closing admonitions for Christian endurance, an example is given of a man who gave up his inheritance for a bowl of beans. Hebrews 12:14-17 gives this advice: *"Make every effort to live in peace with all men and to be holy; without holiness no one will see the Lord. See to it that no one misses the grace of God and that no bitter root grows up to cause trouble and defile many. See that no one is sexually immoral, or is godless like Esau, who for a single meal sold his inheritance rights as the oldest son. Afterward, as you know, when he wanted to inherit this blessing, he was rejected. He could bring about no change of mind, though he sought the blessing with tears."*

We are told in Genesis 25:34 that Esau despised his birthright. Imagine that! To give up your rights as first-born son is no minor thing. The firstborn son would generally receive a double portion of the father's estate since he would become the patriarch of the family after his father passed away. The firstborn would become the executor of the father's estate, and the one to take care of any remaining relatives. For this reason, he would receive a double portion of the inheritance.

Esau gave up that right without so much as a second thought because his stomach was growling, and his younger twin, Jacob offered him a bargain: a bowl of red-bean soup for the rights of the firstborn. Esau's flippant response was, "I am about to die (with hunger) so of what use then is the birthright to me?" Esau traded his inheritance for a bowl of beans!

I wonder how many Christians today have made similar bargains. Too many are ignorant of their inheritance from God, or worse, devil-may-care about the blessings God has promised. It is a tragedy to ignore or perhaps trade away a valuable inheritance. We can easily see the foolishness of doing that kind of thing in the physical realm, but many of us carelessly bypass the full measure of our spiritual inheritance.

The inheritance we focus on here is connected to certain righteous qualities and denied to those with certain unrighteous qualities: The chart below contains 11 verses that cover a comparison between righteous deeds and unrighteous deeds. You will notice that righteous deeds lead to positive consequences related to inheritance, and certain negative deeds lead to negative consequences. Consider the following scriptures and the connection between actions and results.

Text:	Quality or action:	Result:
Mat. 5:5	Meekness	Inherit the earth
Mat. 19:29	Leave family or lands for my sake	Inherit eternal life
Mark 10:17, Luke 18:18	"What must I do"	Inherit eternal life
I Cor. 6:9	Wicked, sexually immoral, idolaters, adulterers, etc.	Will not inherit the kingdom of God
1 Cor. 6:10	Thieves, greedy, drunkards, slanderers, swindlers	Will not inherit the kingdom of God
1 Cor. 15:50	Flesh and blood, perishable	Cannot inherit the kingdom of God
Gal. 5:21	Envy, drunkenness, orgies, and the like	Will not inherit the kingdom of God

Heb. 6:12	Not lazy, but faith and patience	Inherit what has been promised
James 2:5	Poor in the eyes of the world, rich in faith	Inherit the kingdom He promised those who love him
1 Peter 3:9	Not repay evil with evil or insult with insult, but with blessing	Inherit a blessing
Rev. 21:7	He who overcomes	Will inherit all this

What we see in the chart above might lead some to conclude that salvation, and the inheritance that accompanies it, is a matter of works rather than faith. Since so many of the world's religions are works oriented, many wrongly conclude that Christianity is just like everything else in the religious realm. The difference here is that entrance into the kingdom of God comes by faith rather than works of the flesh (Ephesians 2:8-9). Once we are saved apart from our works, God continues to work within us to transform us from carnal "worldlings" into those who share in God's nature.

Peter spoke of this transformation process in 2 Peter 1:3-8, *"His divine power has given us everything we need for life and godliness through our knowledge of him who called us by his own glory and goodness. Through these he has given us his very great and precious promises, so that through them you may participate in the divine nature and escape the corruption in the world caused by evil desires. For this reason make every effort to add to your faith goodness; and to goodness, knowledge; and to knowledge, self-control; and to self control, perseverance; and to perseverance, godliness; and to godliness, brotherly kindness; and to brotherly kindness, love. For if you possess these qualities in increasing measure, they will keep you from being ineffective and unproductive in your knowledge of our Lord Jesus Christ."*

Our entrance into God's kingdom is independent of human merit, but our growth and sanctification into maturity as Christians involves a partnership where God starts and completes the work through the Holy Spirit. We cooperate by entering into the process of discipleship that transforms us from unstable babies into maturing and dedicated followers of Jesus Christ.

Jesus preached about a "straight gate" and a "narrow way" (Matthew 7:13-14). Most people who hear the gospel focus on the gate (entering into salvation), and neglect to learn anything about the way (the process of discipleship that grows us from spiritual infancy into reproducing maturity). What the New Testament teaches about our inheritance takes into account the process of growing in our faith.

In 1 Kings 21, we find an example of a person willing to go to his death defending his rightful inheritance. The man's name is Naboth the Jezreelite, and his inheritance was a vineyard which happened to be located beside the palace of King Ahab of Samaria. King Ahab wanted the vineyard for himself. He offered to switch out properties with Naboth, giving him another piece of land. Then he generously offered to pay for the vineyard in cash. Here was Naboth's response, (vs. 3) *"The Lord forbid me that I should give you the inheritance of my fathers."*

The true value for Naboth was not just the value of the land itself. If that had been the case, he would have agreed to a trade with the king. This was an inheritance that had likely been in the family for generations. This land brought to mind the memories of many ancestors. Naboth did not want to treat an inheritance as just another piece of real estate. He likely wanted to pass it on down to his own heirs. Therefore, he disappointed the powerful king of Samaria. And as we can see in the ending of this story, it was dangerous to disappoint Ahab. Naboth lost his life when Ahab's wicked and conniving wife, Jezebel, hatched a plot to have Naboth killed. The King then seized the vineyard next door.

When we see the way this story turned out, we might shake our heads at a man who forfeits his life to defend his inheritance. We wonder,

"Why not take the deal and save your skin?" But Jews of that day would understand. Inheritance, especially of family land, was no small matter. People in Israel would do whatever it took to preserve the family farm and pass it on to the next generation. The estate was bound with the identity and the honor of the family.

My own family experienced the pain of a lost inheritance. My grandfather, Thurman Skidmore, owned a 110 acre farm not far from the town of Raymond. It had been in the Skidmore family for several generations, and included a two story farm house, a barn, various out-buildings, and a small detached garage. The State in which he lived exercised the right of imminent domain to seize grandpa's land and the land next door to it, which was the property of my Uncle Merle. The state saw the Skidmore land as a great location for an auto test track next to an auto manufacturing plant.

The state paid Grandpa less than $60,000 for the whole farm and instructed them to vacate the premises. The loss of his land was so traumatic that my grandmother had a heart attack and died before the move out date. Grandpa moved out and lived for a while with one of his sons, but he was never the same. Due to dementia, he soon forgot that he had ever married or had children. He was friendly to whoever visited him, but failed to recognize his own children or grand-children as his own kin. In his mind, he still lived as a boy on that family farm that had been commandeered by the State.

My uncle Marston took me by the farm property years later to see what was left of it. The government did not end up using the land for the project they had in mind, so they made money from the land by renting it to other farmers. Homeless vagrants had moved into the farm house and set it on fire, burning it down to the ground. All the other buildings were torn down as well. Two blue spruce trees remained as the only recognizable landmark on what had been the Skidmore farm.

I asked my uncle what would likely have happened if the land had not been taken away. He suggested that one of the grand kids would have inherited it and worked the farm just as Grandpa had done. Then I asked why the family had not sued the State for improper use of the land they had taken. His response was, "How do you sue a state?"

I think back to how meaningful that property was to me as a child growing up near my grandparents, and how devastating it felt to lose an important piece of our family history. From that time on, I was less inclined to develop much of an attachment to houses or land. The demise of family property made the words of a chorus so much more meaningful to me,

> This world is not my home, I'm just a passin' through.
> My treasures are laid up, somewhere beyond the blue.
> The angels beckon me, to heaven's golden shore,
> And I can't feel at home in this world any more.
> (Albert E. Brumley)

As a member of the Skidmore family, I often wish that the family farm could have been preserved so that generations to come could see and enjoy the family homestead. The fact that we were powerless to hold on to that inheritance, is a source of sadness to those who used to play and roam around Grandpa's farm. I can sympathize with how Naboth might have felt when King Ahab offered him a deal for his vineyard. Then I compare Naboth's story to that of Esau. One was willing to die to preserve what the other gave away for a bowl of red beans.

What does it take to defend your inheritance? In Naboth's case it meant refusing to sell his land at any price to anyone. His dedication to his inheritance cost him his life, but he would not sell out. When it comes to physical assets, some say that everyone has a price. Everyone will sell out for the right financial deal. Naboth was an exception to that rule. He understood the value of his inheritance and held on to it with everything he had.

Our spiritual inheritance is much more valuable than any physical asset. It is a treasure to be valued and preserved. We hold on to our inheritance for our own benefit and we hold on to it so we can pass it on. Telling others about our inheritance enables those around us to share in that blessing as well.

Holding on to our inheritance involves such things as "abiding in Christ" (John 15:4-9), and "walking in the Spirit" (Galatians 5:25). By continuing in the way of Christ, we are able to "make our calling and election sure" (2 Peter 1:10). This is the way we guard our inheritance. Hebrews 2:1-3 admonishes, *"We must pay more careful attention, therefore, to what we have heard, so that we do not drift away. For if the message spoken by angels was binding, and every violation and disobedience received its just punishment, how shall we escape if we ignore such a great salvation? ..."* Let us, therefore, pay attention to the wonderful inheritance we have received from our Great God.

After reading about our spiritual inheritance in Christ, how would you rate your own attitude? Would your attitude about the divine inheritance match up closer to that of Naboth or Esau? Are you able to appreciate the value of the inheritance God has provided for you? Will you preserve and defend your inheritance? Are you willing to take inventory of the riches you have inherited because of the mercy and grace of God? Is your faith more than just fire insurance against a bad eternal outcome? Will you appropriate for yourself today what God has appropriated in your behalf in time past? Will you broadcast the blessing to others so they can become joint heirs along with you and Christ?

What do you now understand about your spiritual inheritance, and what will you do about it?

Let us consider once again the prayer of Paul to the Ephesians, *"I keep asking that the God of our Lord Jesus Christ, the glorious Father, may give you the Spirit of wisdom and revelation, so that you may know him better. I pray also that the eyes of your heart may be enlightened in order that you may know the hope to which he has called you, the riches of his glorious inheritance in the saints, and his incomparably great power for us who believe..."* (Ephesians 1:17-19)

Questions to Consider:

1. Why do you think Esau so quickly gave away his birthright (Hebrews 12:16-17)?

2. Studying the verses that attach righteous behavior or attitudes to inheritance, what are we to conclude about our spiritual inheritance?

3. In what way did Naboth behave differently than Esau (1 Kings 21)?

4. What happens if you fail to defend your inheritance?

5. What new lessons have you learned from this study? What does it mean to defend your inheritance?

6. In Hebrews 2:1-3 what does it mean to "drift away" or to "ignore such a great salvation"?

Chapter 13: A Case Study in Dual Inheritance

Key Verse: Luke 15:12, *"The younger one said to his father, 'Father, give me my share of the estate.' So he divided his property between them."*

Luke 15 contains a familiar parable we often call "the prodigal son". We generally focus on the physical side of the prodigal's inheritance. The son demanded his share of the father's estate, and the father complied with the request. What is evident in the story, but rarely emphasized, is the duality of the son's inheritance. When the son demanded his physical inheritance, he showed disdain for an inheritance of greater value, the spiritual inheritance of a loving relationship with his father.

When the son called for his share of the estate, the boy implied a wish that his father were dead. The kind of property divisions he demanded would not usually be made until after the death of the benefactor. The demand was an insult. We discover later in the story that the elder brother was well aware of the insult. The prodigal was not merely leaving home. He was rejecting the entire family. No doubt, Jesus was aware of the emotions he was stirring up as he told this story. He knew that the crowd would tend to empathize with the older brother and despise the younger brother.

In Luke 15:13 we see that the boy squandered his physical inheritance in "wild living". From what is stated in the text we must conclude that the father had put a monetary value on the portion of land the boy would have inherited and gave it to the boy in spendable coinage. It seems the father not only knew what the boy would do with the inheritance, he actually enabled the boy's foolish actions by providing liquidity to the boy's portion of the estate.

These days parents sometimes attempt to protect the estate against foolish liquidation of assets by setting up a trust fund that meters out the assets in periodic dribbles after the child has reached a suitable age. Many parents have savings set up for the child to cover important things like college tuition or the down payment on a car or home. The desire of the parent is to provide for the child's needs while insuring the inheritance is not squandered.

The term "sudden wealth syndrome" has been coined to describe the propensity of lottery winners and inheritors of large estates to spend everything almost overnight. I recall an acquaintance of mine who won a lottery and immediately gave generous portions to various relatives. A year later, a brother who had been given a million dollars requested more. He had gone through his million in less than a year. Rather than being grateful for the original gift, the brother was livid because his sibling would not ante up a second time. This is the end result for many who receive a sudden influx of money, and it was certainly the outcome for the prodigal son.

I suspect that the reckless spending on the part of the prodigal son was indicative of a lack of respect for his family's wealth and, more than that, a lack of respect for his family in general. The cliché, "easy come; easy go," tells only half the story here. The squandering of this family inheritance seems to be powered by a spirit of rebellion and irrational anger. From all appearances, the prodigal set out to purposefully obliterate everything the family had worked so hard to amass. Whatever his intent, the boy achieved this goal in short order. Surely the boy had plenty of help from friends who were all too willing to consume his assets. And just as surely, when the stash was gone, so were the friends.

Jesus added a famine to the picture, making the boy's poverty even more intense. He might have lived off of the kindness of some of his good-time friends, but now everyone around him was hurting, too. No one could afford to be generous. So the boy began to experience genuine need for the first time in his life. Hunger forced him to seek employment, and the famine forced him to take anything he could find.

Once again, Jesus inserted an element guaranteed to arouse emotion on the part of the listeners. His largely Jewish audience would wince at the notion of slopping the hogs. No more un-kosher occupation could be found than this. Naturally, the boy, though a rebel at heart, would be sensitive to the shame attached to such ignoble work. He was hungry enough to eat the garbage he was feeding the pigs, but the text says no one would give him anything to eat.

Jesus said that the boy came to his senses. Indeed! Oh, the blessed education of hunger! Finally, his thoughts turned longingly to home. He recalled that even his father's field hands lived better than this. The boy knew he had burned his bridges behind him. He knew he had trampled upon his status as his father's son. He had squandered his inheritance. Not just the physical inheritance of wealth, but the spiritual inheritance of belonging. The boy had no doubt about how the family would feel about his insult and idiocy.

He was right about the change in his status as an heir. The words of the father to the elder brother in verse 31 of Luke 15 is revealing, *"…everything I have is yours."* It was true that the prodigal would never again inherit a portion of the family's lands. His demand had placed everything that was left in the elder brother's hands. The younger son had kissed his inheritance good-bye.

The prodigal son began to rehearse a speech he would give to the father upon returning home. Since he was no longer worthy to be called "son," he asked to be a hired hand on the farm. Having suffered every imaginable humiliation, this boy was finally humble enough to return home with a different heart. The anger was gone. The envy of the father's wealth had evaporated. Finally, the boy was glad his father was still alive. So how would the father react to the boy's return? For the prodigal son, this was the great unknown.

But Jesus did not keep the listeners in the dark about the father's attitude. The whole time the boy was gone, the father kept a watchful eye on the horizon. Every day, the father watched anxiously for the possibility of the boy's return. The boy was not forgotten or spurned by his dad. I doubt that the crowd hearing the story that day shared the attitude of the father in the parable. Most Jewish fathers, hearing this story, were thinking that the boy deserved whatever pain or deprivation befell him. He had lessons to learn. He deserved his "come-uppins". But this isn't a story about justice. This is a story about mercy.

We see the heart of the father as he scanned the horizon day after day, just in case the boy might appear. Then one day, the father saw his son walking toward him. When the boy was still in the distance, the father ran to his son. He hugged and kissed the boy. The father interrupted the boy's pitiful speech by shouting directives to his servants, "Quick, prepare a banquet! My son is guest of honor!" The father had good cause to tell the errant son a thing or two, but instead he demonstrated his unfaltering love for a son who had been as good as dead and was now alive and back home.

This is where the second inheritance is revealed. The physical inheritance was spent. The spiritual inheritance still remained in full and was freely bestowed on the son by his father. This is an inheritance that was never withdrawn from the prodigal son. This inheritance waited only for the prodigal's return. No bad action on his part could nullify the offer of the spiritual inheritance. This is what he had proved by the rotten things the son did, in his manner of leaving home and in his actions after he left. The elder brother evidently resented the fact that his wayward brother could still inherit his full share of the father's love. But the brother had no power to grant or deny the inheritance. It rested firmly in the hands and heart of the father.

The spiritual inheritance is between father and son. It is kept safe and secure in the heart of the Father where it cannot be corrupted or destroyed. This seems to be the intent of the powerful passage in 1 Peter 1:3-4, *"Praise be to the God and Father of our Lord Jesus Christ! In his great mercy he has given us new birth into a living hope through the resurrection of Jesus Christ from the dead, and into an inheritance that can never perish, spoil or fade—kept in heaven for you..."*

Our glorious inheritance is multifaceted. Physical blessings may be squandered, but our spiritual inheritance is held secure in the Father's heart. We inherit, not through our own merit, but because of the Father's love. Our own failings cannot disqualify us. No one's disapproval can exclude us. Only our own rebellious disbelief can keep us from our rightful inheritance. When we turn to our heavenly Father, his arms are outstretched. He is waiting and watching for us to open our hearts to him so he can pour out the full measure of our glorious spiritual inheritance.

Questions to Consider:

1. The Title of this chapter talks about "dual inheritance." We know the prodigal son was seeking for a physical inheritance, but what was the inheritance the boy did not know about and was not seeking for himself?

2. Why did Jesus take the time to include the older brother in this story? What does his attitude reveal?

3. What do you think finally brought the younger brother to his senses?

4. What speech did he prepare to say to his father, and what did he hope to accomplish by saying those words?

5. What does this story teach about the love of the father for his wayward child?

6. What has God taught us about his own attitude through this amazing parable?

7. Who do you most identify with in the story? The Father? The Prodigal? Or the Elder Brother?

Chapter 14: Our Future Inheritance

Key Verse: Romans 8:18, *"I consider that our present sufferings are not worth comparing with the glory that will be revealed in us."*

Much of our spiritual inheritance benefits us in the here and now. We enjoy the daily benefits of our multifaceted relationship with God, our connection to Christ who is in us just as we are in Him, the presence of the Holy Spirit who is our down payment on all the blessings that are to come. We are also empowered by the new covenant which has replaced the old covenant of laws and rituals, the victorious experience of the overcomers and their great rewards, the continuous blessing of being joint heirs with Christ, the authority of the name of Christ and our ability to use His name in prayer, ministry, and spiritual warfare.

We appropriate our inheritance by faith and by this means we can live daily life in the kingdom of God. We have inherited a life filled with righteousness, peace, and joy in the Holy Spirit. While living in the present, we seek to guard and defend our inheritance against the pressures that would keep us from realizing the treasure that is available to us.

But our glorious spiritual inheritance cannot be entirely contained in the present tense. In fact, that which we experience in present tense is a mere foretaste of what is promised in the future tense. Some of this future inheritance was mentioned in the chapter dealing with rewards enumerated in Revelation chapters 2 and 3. These rewards presuppose the two main elements of our future inheritance: our new resurrection bodies and our new eternal home in heaven.

Resurrection Bodies

In Genesis 3, sin and its curse of death, enters a world that had been perfect for only two short chapters. From that point on we face a planet filled with pain, sickness, suffering, decay, and death. We know that the things we own wear out, break down, or are stolen. Our own bodies show constant evidence of weakness, susceptibility to illness, and the inevitable deterioration of aging. The law of entropy dictates that everything is on a ceaseless voyage from order to chaos. As Christians, our personal and corporate prayers are consistently filled with requests for healing and physical restoration, but we know that even these answered prayers will only give temporary relief.

The New Testament promises a future inheritance. When that inheritance is bestowed, our mortal bodies will be replaced by immortal bodies. The Apostle Paul addressed this matter with the Christians in Corinth when he wrote these words in 1 Corinthians 15:49-53, *"And just as we have borne the likeness of the earthly man, so shall we bear the likeness of the man from heaven. I declare to you, brothers, that flesh and blood cannot inherit the kingdom of God, nor does the perishable inherit the imperishable. Listen, I tell you a mystery: We will not all sleep, but we will all be changed-- in a flash, in the twinkling of an eye, at the last trumpet. For the trumpet will sound, the dead will be raised imperishable, and we will be changed. For the perishable must clothe itself with the imperishable and the mortal with immortality."*

Our eternal bodies will not suffer the kinds of limitations and debilitations common to our fleshly bodies. This is a consolation for any person, but it increases in value to us as our bodies age. For instance, I was 55 when I was told by my doctor that I had gone from borderline diabetes to full-fledged type 2 diabetes. Now I have a handful of pills to take every day, and the need to test my blood sugar levels regularly, not to mention visiting several kinds of specialists annually. With each passing year, it seems, new ailments add to my personal list of physical limitations. For this reason I look forward to a new heavenly body, completely free from physical malady. And, I must admit, it would be great to have a resurrection body with a slim mid-section free of adipose tissue.

A Heavenly Home

When we think of our glorious inheritance, the promise of heaven is probably the first thing that comes to mind. We are more likely to know about our inheritance of a heavenly home than of any other reward. The fact is that many of the rewards we experience before heaven foreshadow the greater inheritance to come. Our close relationship with God will be face-to-face in heaven. We will one day experience, in full, the present fact that we are seated with Christ in heaven. Righteousness, peace, and joy in the Holy Spirit will be unlimited and uninterrupted in our heavenly home.

Jesus taught more about heaven than any other Biblical teacher. In fact, the Old Testament has very little to say about heaven. We rely on New Testament texts for the bulk of what we know about the place described in Revelation as the "New Jerusalem." The New Testament ends with a stirring description of the wonders of heaven.

The details about what is in heaven are glorious, but even more impressive are the details about what is not in heaven. The descriptions of heaven may be hard for us to imagine, but we can instantly comprehend the things that will not be in heaven. The list below is not meant to be exhaustive but merely indicative of what heaven is like.

What is not in heaven:

- No night (darkness) – Revelation 22:5
- No need of the sun or moon for light. Revelation 21:23
- No more seas. Revelation 21:1
- No more curse. Revelation 22:3
- No more death. Revelation 21:4
- No more tears or pain. Revelation 21:4
- No separation from God. Revelation 21:3
- No thirst. Revelation 21:6

- No immorality. Revelation 21:8
- No temple for God and Jesus are the temple. Revelation 21:22
- No unclean thing. Revelation 21:27
- No lying. Revelation 22:15
- No devil. Revelation 20:10

If we were to stop with the first list, it would be enough to give a panorama of the greatness and glory of our future inheritance. But wait! There's more! Let's take a look at what Revelation 21-22 tells us about what is in heaven:

What is in heaven?

- New heaven and new earth. Revelation 21:1
- New Jerusalem adorned as a bride for her husband. Revelation 21:2
- God's presence with mankind (both Father and Son). Revelation 21:3
- All things made new. Revelation 21:5
- The spring and river of the water of life. Revelation 21:6, 22:1
- The church (the bride of the Lamb). Revelation 21:9
- The glory of God. Revelation 21:11
- A high wall and 12 gates that never close. Revelation 21:12-14, 25
- Gold and precious stones. Revelation 21:18-21
- The Lamb's Book of Life. Revelation 21:27
- The throne of God and of the Lamb. Revelation 22:1
- The tree of life. Revelation 22:2
- Eternity (for ever and ever). Revelation 22:5

Of course Heaven can hardly be contained in any mere list. Descriptions of our future home and the gifts and rewards that are promised do little more than whet our appetite to know more. When we look at all the wonderful aspects of heaven we can rejoice in the fact that there is no end to righteousness, peace, and joy in the

Holy Spirit. In this life all good things must come to an end. For every "Hello" there must be a subsequent "Good bye." But the heavenly celebration will never end.

God has promised a future home for his own that can never be fully described in human language. But the caveat here is that heaven is promised to God's own. The future heaven is populated with those whose names are written in the Lamb's Book of Life. Does Christ reign in your heart today? If so, then you are the beneficiary of a glorious inheritance. You know that your reservation in heaven is secure. The Holy Spirit dwells within you as a guarantee of your inheritance.

If you don't have the assurance of that blessed hope, you can do something to change where you stand before God. This entire study has been for the purpose of encouraging those who are God's own. You can belong to God, too. Please don't turn your back on your loving Heavenly Father. Invite Jesus to be your Savior today.

Questions to Consider:

1. What things about heaven did you already know before you read this chapter?
2. What new thing did you learn about heaven from your reading today?
3. What will be the most exciting thing you will enjoy about your new eternal body?
4. Of all the things not found in heaven, which one of them causes you the most joy?
5. Looking at the list of things found in heaven, what is the best thing to you on that list?
6. Though the material in this chapter is about our future inheritance in heaven, how does that aspect of inheritance compare with the many things we inherit now?

Chapter 15: Passing on Our Inheritance

Key Scripture: Proverbs 13:22, *"A good man leaves an inheritance for his children's children…"*

Throughout this book we have examined the riches of our spiritual inheritance as beloved children in God's forever family. We have uncovered the wealth that is ours now and in the ages to come. The reason for taking the time to see all that God has bestowed upon us should be obvious by now. Our inheritance goes far beyond mere entrance into the heavenly gates. Christianity is much more than fire insurance against infernal terrors. God not only adopted us into his family by the completed work of Christ on the cross, He has also planted His divine nature into us thereby giving us His own spiritual DNA (2 Peter 1:2-4).

God has made us joint heirs with Christ. He was the first-fruits of a rich harvest to follow. We are all part of that abundant harvest. We have the privilege to interact directly with Father, Son, and Holy Spirit. No aspect of God has been withheld from us. Our connection with God is both direct and personal. We do not need any human intermediary to represent us before God. No other religion in the world promises the degree of accessibility and interaction that we are privileged to enjoy with our Sovereign God.

Coming to a greater understanding of this truth can encourage and inspire us to cling to our great Provider with obedience and devotion. We do not follow God in order to placate Him with flawless behavior. In truth, we know that despite our flawed actions, we are accepted fully in the Beloved (Ephesians 1:6).

This is quite a departure from the view outsiders commonly hold about Christian faith in God. As Christians, we have no need to behave ourselves into righteousness. Instead, we begin our lives in God's family as fully pardoned, beloved children who have already been declared holy in God's sight. (Ephesians 1:4, Colossians 1:22, Romans 8:1). Our rich inheritance from God, if understood and boldly proclaimed, provides a strong and effective presentation of full salvation in Christ Jesus.

Jesus taught that we are light and salt (Matthew 5:13-16). Consider where our light shines. Where do we display our saltiness? This is part of the legacy for which God placed us on earth.

Furthermore, our inheritance from God is a legacy that we can pass on to others. Proverbs 13:22 reminds us that a good man leaves an inheritance to his children's children. His intention is to have a positive impact on multiple generations to follow. Since a spiritual legacy was given to us, we have a challenge before us to keep the chain of inheritance intact. Knowing the priceless value of our inheritance, we desire to bless others as we have been blessed.

The Old Testament Jews were urged to tell their children about God and his mighty deeds. They were commanded to pass on the words of the law and the stories of God's wondrous works to future generations (Deuteronomy 6:4-9, Psalm 103). We do not live under the dictates of the Levitical Law, but our responsibility to pass on what we have come to know is no less imperative. We show the value of our inheritance by the way we live it, preserve it, protect it, appropriate it, and pass it on to others.

I recall a bumper sticker on a motor home with this message, "We're spending our children's inheritance." Obviously, that was a joke, but I wonder how often it turns out that a person earns or inherits treasure only to spend it all on self. Some may justify their selfish behavior by saying. "I had to earn it myself, and my kids need to earn it themselves." Such short sighted logic fails to see the good that can be done for those in the shadow of your example.

I have led several sessions of Financial Peace University through the years, and I appreciate the words of Dave Ramsey who reminded us that we could literally change the lives of future generations if we pay off debt and build wealth wisely. Susan and I decided when our children were young, that we would do whatever it took to put our children through college. We had seen other people strapped with college loans that took decades to pay off. For that reason, Susan took a full time job with the primary objective of paying for the girl's college bills. We were thankful to be able to provide so that both girls graduated debt free.

While it is true that we need to bless others with our financial resources, it is immeasurably more important that we pass along a spiritual legacy of faith. All the wonderful treasures we have inherited lie beside us, within us, and before us. This amazing spiritual inheritance was not given to us so we could hoard it, but so we could joyfully pass the treasure on to others who come alongside us and who come after us.

This is precisely why God went beyond saving us as individuals, and connected us together within His church. He has built us as living stones into one spiritual house so that we can accomplish together what could not be done individually (1 Peter 2:5, Ephesians 4:11-16). As we enjoy our spiritual inheritance together, we are able to grow into maturity. In this way everyone can rejoice in what God has so generously provided for all of us.

Through the years of my ministry I have seen countless examples of altruism within the church. In the church I'm currently serving, a generous lady chose to provide a scholarship fund for training up preachers. Right now, a young man is in his second year of Christian College because of her generosity. He is not related to her physically, but the spiritual connection they share has produced a legacy that is impacting his life and the lives of everyone he helps in the future. One of our church elders gives time every week to mentor a former prison inmate. His investment of time is producing dividends which are increasingly visible in the life of the one he is mentoring. For decades a group of people in our church have provided Sunday worship services in a local nursing home, ministering to many elderly folks who are so often neglected and alone. These examples could be multiplied by thousands across the nation and the world as God's Church passes along the riches He has provided.

As we conclude this study of our spiritual inheritance, consider what legacy you hope to leave behind? What will you pass on of your practices, priorities, principles, and passion? God has given you a rich and eternal inheritance. Share your treasures with others and leave precious memories that will never be forgotten. "You have freely received; freely give" (Matthew 10:8).

Questions to Consider:

1. Of all the things you have learned from this study, what do you consider to be the greatest aspect of your spiritual inheritance?

2. What element of your spiritual inheritance surprised you the most?

3. What part of your spiritual inheritance gives you the greatest joy and thanksgiving to God for His provision?

4. What examples can you cite from your experiences in the church of observing someone passing on an inheritance to others?

5. What would you most like to pass on to others as a spiritual legacy?

6. What will be the next step you will take to bring that desire into reality? (See question 5)

Appendix A: Inheritance Passages in the New Testament

Inheritance (NIV):

Matthew 25:34, Then the King will say to those on his right, 'Come, you who are blessed by my Father; take your **inheritance**, the kingdom prepared for you since the creation of the world.'

Acts 20:32, Now I commit you to God and to the word of his grace, which can build you up and give you an **inheritance** among all those who are sanctified.

Galatians 3:18, For if the **inheritance** depends on the law, then it no longer depends on a promise; but God in his grace gave it to Abraham through a promise.

Galatians 4:30, But what does the Scripture say? "Get rid of the slave woman and her son, for the slave woman's son will never share in the **inheritance** with the free woman's son."

Ephesians 1:14, ...who is a deposit guaranteeing our **inheritance** until the redemption of those who are God's possession--to the praise of his glory.

Ephesians 1:18, I pray also that the eyes of your heart may be enlightened in order that you may know the hope to which he has called you, the riches of his glorious **inheritance** in the saints...

Ephesians 5:5, For of this you can be sure: No immoral, impure or greedy person--such a man is an idolater--has any **inheritance** in the kingdom of Christ and of God.

Colossians 1:12, ...giving thanks to the Father, who has qualified you to share in the **inheritance** of the saints in the kingdom of light.

Colossians 3:24, ...since you know that you will receive an **inheritance** from the Lord as a reward. It is the Lord Christ you are serving.

Hebrews 9:15, For this reason Christ is the mediator of a new covenant, that those who are called may receive the promised eternal **inheritance**--now that he has died as a ransom to set them free from the sins committed under the first covenant.

Hebrews 11:8, By faith Abraham, when called to go to a place he would later receive as his **inheritance**, obeyed and went, even though he did not know where he was going.

Hebrews 12:16, See that no one is sexually immoral, or is godless like Esau, who for a single meal sold his **inheritance** rights as the oldest son.

1 Peter 1:4, ...and into an **inheritance** that can never perish, spoil or fade--kept in heaven for you,

Inherit (NIV):

Matthew 5:5, Blessed are the meek, for they will **inherit** the earth.

Matthew 19:29, And everyone who has left houses or brothers or sisters or father or mother or children or fields for my sake will receive a hundred times as much and will **inherit** eternal life.

Mark 10:17, As Jesus started on his way, a man ran up to him and fell on his knees before him. "Good teacher," he asked, "what must I do to **inherit** eternal life?"

Luke 10:25, On one occasion an expert in the law stood up to test Jesus. "Teacher," he asked, "what must I do to **inherit** eternal life?"

Luke 18:18, A certain ruler asked him, "Good teacher, what must I do to **inherit** eternal life?"

1 Corinthians 6:9-10, Do you not know that the wicked will not **inherit** the kingdom of God? Do not be deceived: Neither the sexually immoral nor idolaters nor adulterers nor male prostitutes nor homosexual offenders nor thieves nor the greedy nor drunkards nor slanderers nor swindlers will **inherit** the kingdom of God.

1 Corinthians 15:50, I declare to you, brothers, that flesh and blood cannot **inherit** the kingdom of God, nor does the perishable **inherit** the imperishable.

Galatians 5:21, ...and envy; drunkenness, orgies, and the like. I warn you, as I did before, that those who live like this will not **inherit** the kingdom of God.

Hebrews 1:14, Are not all angels ministering spirits sent to serve those who will **inherit** salvation?

Hebrews 6:12, We do not want you to become lazy, but to imitate those who through faith and patience **inherit** what has been promised.

Hebrews 12:17, Afterward, as you know, when he wanted to **inherit** this blessing, he was rejected. He could bring about no change of mind, though he sought the blessing with tears.

James 2:5, Listen, my dear brothers: Has not God chosen those who are poor in the eyes of the world to be rich in faith and to **inherit** the kingdom he promised those who love him?

1 Peter 3:9, Do not repay evil with evil or insult with insult, but with blessing, because to this you were called so that you may **inherit** a blessing.

Revelation 21:7, He who overcomes will **inherit** all this, and I will be his God and he will be my son.

Heir (NIV):

Matthew 21:38, "But when the tenants saw the son, they said to each other, 'This is the **heir**. Come, let's kill him and take his inheritance.'

Mark 12:7, "But the tenants said to one another, 'This is the **heir**. Come, let's kill him, and the inheritance will be ours."

Luke 20:14, "But when the tenants saw him, they talked the matter over. 'This is the **heir**,' they said. 'Let's kill him, and the inheritance will be ours.'

Romans 4:13, It was not through law that Abraham and his offspring received the promise that he would be **heir** of the world, but through the righteousness that comes by faith.

Galatians 4:1, What I am saying is that as long as the **heir** is a child, he is no different from a slave, although he owns the whole estate.

Galatians 4:7, So you are no longer a slave, but a son; and since you are a son, God has made you also an **heir**.

Hebrews 1:2, ...but in these last days he has spoken to us by his Son, whom he appointed **heir** of all things, and through whom he made the universe.

Hebrews 11:7, By faith Noah, when warned about things not yet seen, in holy fear built an ark to save his family. By his faith he condemned the world and became **heir** of the righteousness that comes by faith.

Heirs (NIV):

Acts 3:25, And you are **heirs** of the prophets and of the covenant God made with your fathers. He said to Abraham, 'Through your offspring all peoples on earth will be blessed.'

Romans 4:14, For if those who live by law are **heirs**, faith has no value and the promise is worthless,

Romans 8:17, Now if we are children, then we are **heirs**--**heirs** of God and co-**heirs** with Christ, if indeed we share in his sufferings in order that we may also share in his glory.

Galatians 3:29, If you belong to Christ, then you are Abraham's seed, and **heirs** according to the promise.

Ephesians 3:6, This mystery is that through the gospel the Gentiles are **heirs** together with Israel, members together of one body, and sharers together in the promise in Christ Jesus.

Titus 3:7, ...so that, having been justified by his grace, we might become **heirs** having the hope of eternal life.

Hebrews 6:17, Because God wanted to make the unchanging nature of his purpose very clear to the **heirs** of what was promised, he confirmed it with an oath.

Hebrews 11:9, By faith he made his home in the promised land like a stranger in a foreign country; he lived in tents, as did Isaac and Jacob, who were **heirs** with him of the same promise.

1 Peter 3:7, Husbands, in the same way be considerate as you live with your wives, and treat them with respect as the weaker partner and as **heirs** with you of the gracious gift of life, so that nothing will hinder your prayers.

Heritage: (KJV)

1 Peter 5:3, Neither as being lords over *God's* **heritage**, but being ensamples to the flock.

About the Author:

Ed Skidmore has been in church related ministry for over 40 years. He has served churches in Kansas, Missouri, New Mexico, and Texas, and ministered in Mexico, Australia, India, Russia, and Kenya. After 13 years in youth ministry, the Skidmores came to San Antonio to begin ministry with the Castle Hills Christian Church. Ed has been with this congregation for about 28 years. He has earned degrees from Ozark Christian College ('72, BSL), California Graduate School of Theology ('83, MA), and Vision International University ('01, D.Min.). Ed is a trustee with Colegio Biblico in Eagle Pass, TX, President of H.O.T.E.A. (Heart of Texas Evangelistic Assn. which plants churches in central Texas), and has broadcast his preaching on KSLR radio station for the past eleven years. Since his graduation from VIU, Ed has been teaching part time classes for the San Antonio campus of Vision International School of Ministry.

A Place at My Father's Table is a devotional book Ed published in 2010. This paperback book is available on Barnes and Noble and Amazon web sites. (ISBN 978-0-557-46831-7)

You're Old Enough to Know is a children's book written by Susan Skidmore to tell her grandchildren about their relationship with God. This is the link to her paperback book on line: http://www.bookemon.com/book-profile/you-re-old-enough-to-know/213118

You may contact Ed Skidmore by phone at 210-464-8684 or e-mail him at edskidmore@sbcglobal.net Write to him at Ed Skidmore 12331 Autumn Vista Dr. San Antonio, TX. 78249. Ed is available for preaching or conducting a seminar on the material included in this book.

www.ingramcontent.com/pod-product-compliance
Lightning Source LLC
LaVergne TN
LVHW051645080426
835511LV00016B/2510